The Poetry of JOHN BERRYMAN

Kennikat Press
National University Publications
Literary Criticism Series

General Editor
John E. Becker
Fairleigh Dickinson University

\

Gary Q. Arpin

The Poetry of
JOHN BERRYMAN

National University Publications
KENNIKAT PRESS // 1978
Port Washington, N. Y. // London

Manufactured in the United States of America

Published by
Kennikat Press Corp.
Port Washington, N. Y. / London

Library of Congress Cataloging in Publication Data

Arpin, Gary Q
   The poetry of John Berryman.

   (Kennikat Press national university publications)
(Literary criticism series)
   Bibliography: p.
   Includes index.
   1. Berryman, John, 1914–1972–Criticism and
interpretation. I. Title.
PS3503.E744Z56   811'.5'4   77-8542
ISBN 0-8046-9205-X

TO SUSAN

ACKNOWLEDGMENTS

Parts of this book were originally published in a different form in *John Berryman Studies* and as *Master of the Baffled House: The Dream Songs of John Berryman.* I am grateful to the Rook Press for permission to reprint them. Alan Williamson and J. C. Levenson read this study in an earlier state and made many helpful suggestions, for which I am deeply grateful. I would also like to thank Ernest Stefanik for his detailed and useful comments. Needless to say, all errors of fact and interpretation are mine.

CONTENTS

The Poetry of JOHN BERRYMAN

INTRODUCTION

To say that John Berryman's poetry is controversial is to state the obvious. Few poets—and none that I can think of since Pound—have aroused such varying and often violent responses. A. Alvarez has written that one either loves or loathes Berryman's work, and that seems to be the case. This should not be a matter of great surprise. For one thing, Berryman's work—especially *The Dream Songs*—is difficult, difficult in a way that most recent poetry is not. At a time when American poetry is moving away from the Eliotic modern, Berryman's work seems to be a throwback, if a self-conscious one, to an earlier age, bringing poetry, to paraphrase Williams's remarks on *The Waste Land*, back into the classroom. The notes to *Homage to Mistress Bradstreet* are perhaps one of the clearest examples of this; appropriate, of course, for an historical poem, but nevertheless self-consciously archaic, if one can use the word in this context, and at the same time, in their repetition of our most famous modern poem's idiosyncrasy—trademark, really—a bit daring. Moreover, although the notes to *Homage* are useful, there is a certain coyness about some of them. Berryman chose, for example, to annotate the line "Our chopping scores my ears" by defining "chopping": "disputing, snapping, haggling; axing." The pun, absolutely necessary for an understanding of the use of "scores," is indicated only by the semicolon. The line is not really annotated, nor is the definition intended as annotation ("chopping" in both its senses is not, after all, an unfamiliar word). Rather, the line is simply brought to the reader's attention; the reader must do the rest of the work himself.

This is only a minor example of a tendency in much of Berryman's mature work which in the best light might be called reticence, in the

3

worst light gamesmanship—a certain toying with the reader. Berryman spoke in interviews of his "trade secrets," and implied that there were secret meanings in *The Dream Songs* that would challenge scholars for years. His work is highly allusive, and he obviously enjoyed this aspect of the difficulty of his work, as lines from *The Dream Songs* indicate:

> I feel the end is near
> & strong of my large work, which will appear,
> and baffle everybody.

This is partially a way of poking fun at the literary establishment, a *blague* directed at the academic community with which Berryman enjoyed a distinct love-hate relationship (compare his portrait of the MLA convention in *77 Dream Songs*). More frequently, though, the allusiveness of Berryman's work is intended to serve a serious function. Berryman was an enormously well-read man, and in his work, especially *The Dream Songs*, he used that knowledge both to create a world and to give the effect of a man ransacking our culture in an attempt to find a way of living in that world. This is not a new use of allusion, obviously; it is firmly in the modernist tradition. The effect of both the playful and the serious uses of allusion, however, has been harmful in some cases, irritating some readers and obscuring more important aspects of his work. *The Dream Songs* is not an intellectual game, but Berryman managed to convince several critics that it was. "After working out the double crostics," wrote Mary Curran of *77 Dream Songs*, "there is only the feeling of dissipation and boredom."[1]

Let us add a further element of difficulty before going on: style. The words "Berryman's style" call up a host of adjectives: idiosyncratic, eccentric, quirky, willed, perverse, in ascending order of disapproval. Style: a use of language that so impresses itself upon the mind that subject and meaning are all but lost. Randall Jarrell's early criticism, in a review of *The Dispossessed,* was prescient: "Doing things in a style all its own sometimes seems the primary object of the poem, and its subject gets a rather spasmodic and fragmentary treatment."[2] The quotation, selectively applied to Berryman's work, even his major work, is accurate—most accurate when the verse is weakest, for the assumption behind the criticism is that style is not intended to hide meaning but to express it, an assumption with which I agree.

But perhaps that assumption is not accurate, at least in regard to *The Dream Songs*. One of the most frequently expressed negative criticisms of Berryman's work is that both his allusiveness and his style are veils which hide a lack of substance. Peter Dale, for example, in an article on

His Toy, His Dream, His Rest, notes that he "share[s] the modern fear of 'being taken for a ride,'"[3] and comes to the conclusion that that is exactly what Berryman is doing to us, making us believe that we are reading important poetry when we are actually reading very ordinary, even simple-minded work. "By his bag of syntactical tricks which defy usage in an unprecedented way Berryman has deliberately jammed the reader's equipment for tone-detection. . . . Yet underneath the modernistic appearance of the poem runs a very traditional, even hackneyed subject matter." Dale concludes that Berryman has skillfully hidden the fact that "five Berrymans might not add up to one poet."[4]

Behind this argument lies the notion that Berryman's work is not what it appears to be. Berryman's admirers disagree with Dale's estimation of Berryman's talent, but frequently agree that his work only masquerades as modernist. Martin Dodsworth, for example, in *The Survival of Poetry,* finds Berryman's major work to be an attack on "Literature," that is, modernist literature in the Symbolist tradition, a literature divorced from life. What is centrally important about *The Dream Songs* is that "despite all appearances, these poems are not hermetic in intention; they seek to *expose* the poet's most remote level of consciousness, to present the reader with the kind of experiences Berryman believes and feels to be behind the superficies of life, but which we are ordinarily content to ignore."[5] This emphasis on experience in the poem proves it to be anti-Symbolist, despite its surface resemblance to a work in the Symbolist tradition. This is the other side of Dale's coin. The poem appears to be modernist, but the style is not explicable by ordinary means. Therefore, the style must serve some other, extraordinary purpose. In Dale's view, it serves to obscure a lack of substance. In Dodsworth's view, the language of the poem is intended to emphasize the importance of experience. What Mr. Dodsworth calls "the *superfluous oddity*" of Berryman's style "is calculated, I think, on the supposition that what is superfluous to the conventional demands of literature may establish a means of personal expression and communication with the reader, something that cannot, as yet, be contaminated by the student's desire to incorporate all literature into some vast and inoffensive system of conventions."[6]

"Superfluous oddity," in the example that Mr. Dodsworth discusses (dream song 33), refers principally to the use of "ah" and "ha," especially their emphatic use as rhyme words. It is not necessary to posit a new poetic to come to terms with this oddity, however. In song 33, the *ah*s and *ha*s are the outbreak of Henry's own powerful emotions aroused by the story of Alexander and Clitus; both the violence and the form it takes of chopping are aspects of Henry's own character that he can barely control, as song 29 makes clear. They are thus not superfluous here; they are rather an indication of the enormous difficulty Henry is having in telling the story. The oddity comes principally from not reading the song as part of a larger whole. I must hasten to add here that I don't think every sample of distorted or mannered language can be justified, or seen as adding to the poem. When such distortions cannot be justified, it seems to me, the language has failed; I do not think that it is necessary (or reasonable) to make of these failures a success. Berryman was a daring poet who pushed the language to its limits and sometimes beyond the limits.

Mr. Dodsworth is, I think, essentially correct when he says that *The Dream Songs* is intimately connected with life, is about living, is, to use Berryman's description of Crane's poetry, *"said for use."* But by equating "Symbolist" with "ideality" and "divorced from life," and *The Dream Songs* with "experience" or "real life," Mr. Dodsworth oversimplifies. In throwing out the bathwater of Symbolist ideality (if indeed that is to be thrown out while discussing Berryman's work), he also throws out a rather substantial baby in the form of Symbolist notions of language in poetry and the image of the poet.

Again, I do not think we need to go to such lengths. I do not think *The Dream Songs* is a radical break with the Symbolist tradition any more than I think it is a radical break from Berryman's earlier poetry. There are some important differences between Berryman's work and the work of the Symbolist and modernist poets who wrote before him, and there are some crucial differences between his major work and his earlier work; but there are also important similarities, ones that should not be ignored. Berryman was, in fact, always a modernist poet, although at different stages in his career different aspects of that modernism were of primary importance to him. The history of his career may indeed be seen as an attempt, or a series of attempts, to discover which aspects of what we have long called the tradition were appropriate to his own vision. And the two things which come immediately to mind, for they were the two areas that were of greatest importance to Berryman's work, are language and the image of the poet.

The origins of Berryman's style have been the subject of a great deal of speculation, largely in terms of a search for a presiding influence. It is not unreasonable to look for such an influence. Berryman's early work was so heavily indebted to the work of Yeats and Auden, and Berryman was always such a bookish poet, that we can expect to find important stylistic influences on his major work as well. Hopkins is most frequently mentioned in this context, although Berryman denied that Hopkins had much influence on him. Cummings has also been men-

tioned, as have Dylan Thomas, Crane (Hart and Stephen), and Stevens.
I would add Milton and especially, as I note in my discussion of *Berry-man's Sonnets*, Tristan Corbière, whose work Berryman was reading
during the time of his own greatest stylistic development in the mid-
1940s. Here is Huysmans's description of Corbière:[7]

> The author was talking negro, using a sort of telegram language, pass-
> ing all bounds in the suppression of verbs, affecting a ribald humor, con-
> descending to quips and quibbles only worthy of a commercial traveller
> of the baser sort; then, in a moment, in this tangle of ludicrous conceits,
> of smirking affectation, would rise a cry of acute pain, like a violoncello
> string breaking.

This is apt, not because Berryman, knowing the quotation (as he doubt-
less did), modelled his own style on it (as he doubtless did not: what
poet models his style on a single quotation from anybody?), but be-
cause it points up a similarity of purpose in the style of the two writers.
Each writer expanded the language to its breaking point (and sometimes
beyond) in order to say things that could not ordinarily be said, with
an intensity with which they could not ordinarily be said.
What poet models his style on a quotation? Berryman provided a
quotation in *Love & Fame*, from R. P. Blackmur, one that points in
the same direction as that from Huysmans:[8]

> "The art of poetry
> is amply distinguished from the manufacture of verse
> by the animating presence in the poetry
> of a fresh idiom: language
>
> so twisted & posed in a form
> that it not only expresses the matter in hand
> but adds to the stock of available reality."

Berryman remarked, "I was never altogether the same man after *that*,"
and so perhaps he wasn't, although the poetry he wrote for ten years
after reading the quotation shows little evidence of it. The point here
is that Berryman's style evolved not just through the reading and influ-
ence of a few other poets, but in response to an aesthetic implicitly
accepted, but never explicitly expressed, the aesthetic of Symbolism,
with its insistence on creating a new language that, in Rimbaud's words,
"would be of the soul, for the soul, containing everything, smells, sounds,
colors; thought latching onto thought and pulling."[9] In this context, I
mean by "aesthetic of Symbolism" not the idealistic foundation for that
aesthetic, but the necessity it imposes of expanding the language, and the

technical liberation that it implies. There is a certain amount of the idealist-aesthete in Berryman, especially, as we shall see, in his early work, but in his major work he is, as Mr. Dodsworth quite correctly points out, concerned above all with living in the world. The language that he found, which we could well describe as containing everything—even some things which some Symbolists would have excluded—served as a means of describing and living with the absurdity and pain of that world.

Berryman's style—but not his interest in style—changed greatly over the course of his career; his thematic concerns changed to a lesser extent. His subject was, as he described Pound's subject matter, "the life of the modern poet," and virtually everything he wrote revolved around that theme. Berryman's image of the poet, though, changed through the years. The poet figure of the early poems is usually sensitive, committed, alienated, and above all aloof, as in "A Poem for Bhain":[10]

> Although the relatives in the summer house
> Gossip and grumble, do what relatives do,
> Demand, demand our eyes and ears, demand us,
>
> You and I are not precisely there
> As they require: heretics, we converse
> Alert and alone, as over a lake of fire
>
> Two white birds following their profession
> Of flight, together fly, loom, fall and rise,
> Certain of the nature and station of their mission.
>
> So by the superficial and summer lake
> We talk, and nothing that we say is heard,
> Neither by the relatives who twitter and ache
>
> Nor by any traveller nor by any bird.

This is the poem of a young man. It appeared in Berryman's 1942 *Poems*, which was dedicated to Bhain Campbell, a young friend of Berryman's who had shortly before died of cancer, the first of Berryman's poet friends to die tragically. At the time the poem was written, Berryman was launching a promising career—he was teaching, writing poetry, had been poetry editor of the *Nation*. In this context, we can perhaps understand the aloofness: what would such an imminently successful, such an aesthetic young man have to do with the "twitter" of provincial parents?

But "A Poem for Bhain" is also obviously the work of a poet under the influence of the idealistic aspects of the Symbolist tradition, inhabiting a realm too rarefied for the gross sensibilities of others. In fact, although the poem doubtless grew out of Berryman's experience, it is so unoriginal, so much a Symbolist poem, that, lost in a crowd of poems on the same subject, it loses its impact.

This aspect of the Symbolist tradition Berryman gradually came to reject. Berryman became more proficient technically, his work became more ambitious, and his image of the poet, although it never lost its connection with certain of the Symbolists' images of the poet (most notably the images of Rimbaud and Corbière), became more complex, more interesting and—most important—more intimately connected with the difficulty of living in the world. In work written a few years after "A Poem for Bhain," the poet's sensitivity and imagination still mark him as different from the rest of us, but his task is no longer pictured as conversing over a lake of fire as in the earlier poem, but understanding and dealing with our common lot. "The Traveller," for example, published in *Poetry* in 1948, is still conventional—too conventional, with its overused images of travelling and alienation—but it gives us a modified image of the poet:[11]

> They pointed me out on the highway, and they said
> "That man has a curious way of holding his head."
> . . . .
> I took the same train that the others took,
> To the same place. Were it not for that look
> And those words, we were all of us the same.
> I studied merely maps. I tried to name
> The effects of motion on the travellers.
> I watched the couple I could see, the curse
> And blessings of that couple. . . .

The poem is not very much more original than "A Poem for Bhain," but the poet figure here is more interesting than in the earlier poem. He is still apart from the rest of the world, his fellow travellers, but he does not have the disdain toward others that was evidenced in his attitude toward the relatives in the earlier poem. His work is not intended to be restricted to the special few; his subject is "The effects of motion on the travellers," our curses and blessings.

There is much in this image of the poet that would remain as a part of Berryman's later work. Berryman's later poet figures—especially, of course, Henry—tell our story, indeed live our story, but remain rejected by the rest of us, apart from us, *poètes maudits* who find it increasingly difficult to find anything that makes the suffering worthwhile.

Berryman's style, as I have noted, derived from the Symbolist aesthetic, with the very important difference that it was intended to create a language that would enable us to express and thus survive, perhaps even triumph over, the absurdity and pain of our lives. Berryman's suffering poet figure is the result of a similar transformation of an element of the Symbolist tradition. He undergoes the suffering that Rimbaud said the poet should undergo, hoping to find not so much the "unknown" or some ideal realm but a strategy for living in a world filled with all-too-real difficulties. In "World Telegram" Berryman had written:[12]

> News of one day, one afternoon, one time.
> If it were possible to take these things
> Quite seriously, I believe they might
> Curry disorder in the strongest brain,
> Immobilize the most resilient will,
> Stop trains, break up the city's food supply,
> And perfectly demoralize the nation.

In his later poetry, not so easily able to remove himself from the news and the threat of madness, Berryman's poet does indeed take such things quite seriously and faces the resultant disorders of the brain. The attempts to deal with "these things," the emergency adaptations of the Symbolist notions of the poet and of language recorded in Berryman's work—especially *Homage* and *The Dream Songs*—are what make Berryman's poetry memorable. The problem is living in the world, a problem that became in Berryman's work increasingly insistent, increasingly intense.

The solution to this problem that Berryman discovered or relied on in much of his work was nominally quite simple, and derived from his reading of Freud—a realization of the importance of love and work. "Love" is used here chiefly in the Freudian sense of "aim-inhibited love," love which binds families and members of a community together. Libidinal love in Berryman's work is a part of the problem, not the solution. Thus, Mistress Bradstreet, after her flirtation with the poet, moves from one form of love to the other:[13]

> Evil dissolves, & love, like foam;
> that love. Prattle of children powers me home.

The "typical" Berryman poem presents a character radically at odds with his environment who, through a process of suffering and self-examination, comes to a realization of the importance of either love or work or both. In both cases it is the character's responsibility to the culture which is rescued from the threats of irresponsibility (on the personal level, usually sex, drink, aggression or the desire for death; on the cultural level, aggression in any number of forms). Stated in other terms, Berryman's characters go through a process of rebellion and submission, finding, however, in that submission a means of triumph. The world doesn't change (or changes in only relatively minor ways), but the character finds a satisfactory means of adapting to it. Mistress Bradstreet, Henry, and the Berryman of the late poems submit to the needs (and joys) of the family and the will of God.

This is grossly oversimplified, of course, and stated so simply leaves out much of what makes Berryman's poetry valuable. For such simple solutions are not and cannot be arrived at simply, and it is the presentation of the enormous and complex difficulties, caused by both internal and external factors, that distinguishes Berryman's work: "Henry in trouble whirped out lonely whines." I hope, in the following study, to make a little clearer both the whines and the whirping.

1

THE EARLY POEMS
AND *THE DISPOSSESSED*

John Berryman was born John Smith on 25 October 1914 in McAlester, Oklahoma. His father, John Allyn Smith, was a banker, and his mother, the former Martha Little, was a schoolteacher. Later that year they moved across the state to Anadarko, a town of 3,000 in southwestern Oklahoma, where they lived until John was ten. In 1924 the family—John's parents, John, and his brother Jefferson—moved to Tampa, Florida. The move did not seem to help the Smiths' marriage. John's father, afraid that his wife would leave him, periodically threatened suicide, his favorite threat being that he would swim out into the Gulf with John under his arm. A few months before John turned twelve, his father shot himself outside John's window. Perhaps no other single event affected Berryman's verse as much as that suicide. It was a profound introduction to what Berryman was later to call "the epistemology of loss," and became the thematic center of much of his later work.

After his father's death John's mother moved the family to New York, where she married another banker, John Angus McAlpin Berryman. Berryman legally adopted both John and Jefferson. John, now John Berryman, took on his new father's name with a vengeance. Throughout his years at Columbia he signed his work either John McAlpin Berryman or John A. McAlpin Berryman, although the switch, or the identity problem it was evidence of, clearly bothered him:[1]

> I stumble strangely over my name
> In the level of speech.
> Use and time should teach
> A fluency of step: came
> Nor comes the sound within my reach.

After public elementary school on Long Island and four years at Kent School, a high-church Episcopalian school in Connecticut, Berryman attended Columbia University, graduating in 1936. His closest friend on the faculty was Mark Van Doren, to whom Berryman later dedicated *His Toy, His Dream, His Rest.* Berryman was active in the student literary societies at Columbia, publishing verse in the *Columbia Review* and *Columbia Poetry,* and winning several prizes for his work. He published in a national magazine for the first time on 10 July 1935. The magazine was the *Nation,* with which Van Doren had long been associated. The poem was a short elegy on the death of Robinson, "Note on E. A. Robinson":[2]

> He was forever walking
> A little north
> To watch the bare words stalking
> Stiffly forth,
> Frozen as they went
> And flawless of heart within without comment.

The poem recalls Robinson's "New England," "Here where the wind is always north-north-east / And children learn to walk on frozen toes." Robinson's sonnet develops by a process of ironic expansion—the New Englanders' "envied" opposites, "who boil elsewhere with such a lyric yeast / Of love" are, at the end of the octave, "Still clamoring where the chalice overflows / And crying wildest who have drunk the least." The emotions of the New Englanders themselves are described in the sestet:

> Passion is here a soilure of the wits,
> We're told, and Love a cross for them to bear;
> Joy shivers in the corner where she knits
> And Conscience always has the rocking-chair,
> Cheerful as when she tortured into fits
> The first cat that was ever killed by Care.

"The sonnet," Berryman had written earlier, "inclines to elaboration."[3] In his six-line "Note" Berryman contracts the terms of the sonnet, and finds the ground between the contrasting ironic descriptions for Robinson and his "bare words": "flawless of heart within without comment." He said much the same thing in prose a few months later in a review of Robinson's *King Jasper:* "Except in a few lyrics, melody has never been a characteristic of his work; here he has pared away all but appropriate and emphatic rhythm. The plan of the poem is very simple and compar-

atively little symbolism is employed. . . . This is the bare statement
toward which he has been working."[4] The "Note on E. A. Robinson"
clearly has over this description what Berryman was later to describe
as the advantage of verse over a prose paraphase:[5]

If to be direct, concrete, compact, is a virtue for the subject as it is here
conceived, the verse has the advantage. In the process of translation the
particular irony and wit escaped; the abruptness of juxtaposition and the
violence were lost.

The poem, indeed, is a quite appropriate beginning for a poet who was
later to be known for the compactness of his verse, the abruptness of
his juxtapositions.

"Note on E. A. Robinson" is probably the best of Berryman's student
work. The choice of subject, however, is not unusual. Although he later
wrote, "I wrote mostly about death,"[6] many of the poems Berryman
published as a student in the *Columbia Review* and *Columbia Poetry*
are about poets or poetry: "Ars Poetica," "Blake," "Elegy: Hart Crane,"
"To an Artist Beginning Her Work." The author of *Homage to Mistress
Bradstreet* was writing about poets very early on. Indeed, Berryman the
student was, Mark Van Doren has written, "first and last a literary youth:
all of his thought sank into poetry, which he studied and wrote as if
there were no other exercise for the human brain. Slender, abstracted,
he lived one life alone, and walked with verse as in a trance."[7] The most
important verse Berryman was walking with at the time was that of
the young W. H. Auden. Berryman later wrote, "I recognized Auden at
once as a new master, / I was by then a bit completely with it."[8] Most
of "Ars Poetica," for example, recalls Auden's early use of dimeter:[9]

> Thus the design
> Is delicate:
>
> Does not record
> In word
> The sequence of scene
> Or scheme of emotion:
> The blade cuts clean
> Cross section in motion,
> Being in one the all
> And thin detail
> Where slow eyes fail
> And steel is tall.

Berryman had doubtless read works of Auden's like "This Lunar Beauty,"
and was attempting to make them his own. This is common among young

poets, of course, but this mixture of the personal and the literary continued to be an important aspect of Berryman's mature work. Much is made of Berryman as an autobiographical poet, but it must be remembered that his reading was frequently as important as his experience. Berryman later turned to Auden not for his form, but for his tone, and Auden's political poems were the basis for some of Berryman's least successful work.

Not all of the student verse is about poetry, of course, or in the style of Auden. Berryman experimented with theme and form a great deal as a student. In the rather nice Imagistic "Trophy," for instance, he wrote on the subject that was to recur constantly in his work—his father's suicide:[10]

> On a winter night
> The cold is apt to awaken
> Ambiguous memory: a man who is gone
>
> Who has not moved
> Heart nor made a gesture this
> Nine years of peace constructing calm
>
> Throws up a hand
> Where a bird sings in
> An ash in spring, a shadow in the sun.

In this poem, as in much of Berryman's later work, winter is the season of spiritual desolation. It is perhaps especially appropriate in the work of a man who spent his childhood in the Deep South, coming north only after his father had left him. Whatever the reason, it is the season of many of the most striking poems in *The Dispossessed* and much of *The Dream Songs*.

During his senior year Berryman had won the Kellet Fellowship at Columbia. So in the late summer of 1936, after his graduation, he went to Clare College, Cambridge, to continue his studies. In 1937 he was an Oldham Shakespeare Scholar at Clare College, and in 1938 he received a B.A. from Cambridge. At Cambridge the Auden influence was tempered by that of Yeats, especially Yeats's meditative-descriptive lyrics. The eight-line stanza Yeats used in "In Memory of Major Robert Gregory" and other poems fascinated Berryman, and he experimented with the form a great deal, not only at Cambridge but for many years thereafter. The stanza form of *Homage to Mistress Bradstreet* is one of the results of that experimentation. He was also fond of a six-line stanza form, probably derived from the early verse of his Cambridge friend Dylan Thomas,[11] to which, of course, he was also to return in later verse. The two forms are used in nine of the 1940 "Twenty Poems," and in thirty-one of the forty-nine poems in *The Dispossessed.* "Yeats," Berryman later wrote, "somehow saved me from the then crushing influences of Ezra Pound and T. S. Eliot—luckily, as I now feel—but he could not teach me to sound like myself (whatever that was) or tell me what to write about."[12]

Sounding like himself was one of Berryman's greatest difficulties, and it could be argued that the influences of Yeats and especially Auden were just as crushing to the young poet as the influences of Eliot and Pound would have been. Influences are crushing only when the poet does not rise above them. Lowell's early work, although heavily influenced, is still important because he made of the influences something that was his own. Berryman's early work—up to about 1946—is promising and accomplished, but aside from a few anthology pieces is rarely more than that.

Subject matter was not difficult for Berryman to find. By 1938, after "extended visits to France and Germany, especially one of the Nazi strongholds, Heidelberg,"[13] and with the example of Auden's work before him, Berryman was writing poems like "Letter to His Brother," which, despite its influences, contains the seed of Berryman's own mature work:[14]

> The night is on these hills, and some can sleep.
> Some stare into the dark, some walk.
> Only the sound of glasses and of talk,
> Of crackling logs, and of a few who weep,
> Comes on the night wind to my waking ears.
> Your enemies and mine are still,
> None works upon us either good or ill:
> Mint by the stream, tree-frogs, are travellers.
>
> What shall I say for anniversary?
> At Dachau many blows forbid
> And Becket's brains upon the pavement spread
> Forbid my trust, my hopeful prophecy.
> Prediction if I make, I violate
> The just expectancy of youth
> And yet you know as well as I the tooth
> Sunk in our heels, the latest guise of fate.
>
> When Patrick Barton chased the murderer
> He heard behind him in the wood
> Pursuit, and suddenly he knew he fled:
> He was the murderer, the others were
> His vigilance. But when he crouched behind
> A tree, the tree moved off and left
> Him naked while the chase came on; he laughed
> And like a hound he leapt out of his mind.

I wish for you—the moon was full, is gone—
Whatever comfort can be got
From the violent world our fathers bought,
For which we pay with fantasy at dawn,
Dismay at noon, fatigue, horror by night.
May love, or its image in work,
Bring you that dignity to know the dark
And so to gain responsible delight.

The stanza is Yeatsian, the tone of despair Audenesque. (When Berryman revised the poem for *The Dispossessed*, he made the tone even more despairing. The "comfort" of line 26 became "bargain," and "that dignity" of line 31 became "the brazen luck.") The ideas in the poem, however, were to be important to Berryman for the rest of his career. In the words of "The Possessed," "this is what you inherited"—the poet has been thrust into a violent world in which he must try to find a responsible way of life. The immediate threat to "responsible delight" here, of course, is Hitler. Berryman's visits to Germany had made him very aware of the Nazi threat. But Hitler is only "the latest guise of fate." The blows at Dachau are essentially the same as those that "Becket's brains upon the pavement spread"—both forbid the poet's "hopeful prophecy." While occupied with the Nazi horror, Berryman is preoccupied with what he called in a poem written at about the same time "our twilight universal curse." This is the capacity for evil which is consistently associated with darkness:[15]

Cedars and the westward sun.
The darkening sky. A man alone
Watches beside the fallen wall
The evening multitudes of sin
Crowd in upon us all.

Thus, since we all share this capacity, the danger implied in the Patrick Barton stanza of "Letter to His Brother": while chasing the latest murderer, we may find him to be ourselves—a chase that ends in madness. (We are brought to the brink of just that madness in "The Dispossessed," written about Hiroshima). In "Letter to His Brother" the twilight has already passed: "The night is on these hills." By the time we reach the last stanza, even the little light the moon had provided is gone. In this poem, and, as we shall see, in virtually all of Berryman's other work, the means of dealing with this darkness are provided by the difficult pair of love and work:

> May love, or its image in work,
> Bring you that dignity to know the dark
> And so to gain responsible delight.

In its theme, images, and even at times style ("prediction if I make, I violate / The just expectancy of youth"), "Letter to His Brother" points forward to Berryman's later work. Nevertheless, it is not a completely successful poem. Its despair is too conventionally literary. The moon, the night, the violent world are not transformed by Berryman into anything more than literary counters skillfully moved into place.

Berryman left New York for Cambridge as a promising young poet. When he returned to New York in 1938, he had a portfolio of some very accomplished verse. Although he had published little while at Cambridge, he made up for it upon his return, publishing a great deal both in small literary magazines and annuals like the *Southern Review, Kenyon Review,* and *New Directions,* and in the more literate national magazines like the *Nation* and the *New Republic.* He also began his peripatetic teaching career, teaching at St. John's College in Maryland, Wayne University in Detroit, and at Harvard College. In 1939 and 1940 he was poetry editor for the *Nation.*

In 1940 James Laughlin brought out the first of his *Five Young American Poets* series, devoted to poets who had not yet published volumes of their own. The first volume gave about forty pages each to Berryman, Mary Barnard, W. R. Moses, George Marion O'Donnell, and Randall Jarrell. Each section contained, in addition to the selection of verse, a portrait and biographical sketch of the poet, a reproduction of a holograph of one poem, and a "Note on Poetry." The volume was generally received as "promising" by the reviewers, most of whom singled out Berryman and Jarrell for special praise. The Yeats influence on Berryman was noted by many.

Berryman's selection "Twenty Poems" contained some very fine work. Besides "Letter to His Brother" he included "The Statue," "Winter Landscape," "World Telegram," and "The Return" (which became "The Possessed" in 1948)—all very impressive poems. He also included "Desires of Men and Women," "On the London Train," "Parting as Descent," "The Disciple," "Conversation," and "Caravan," all of which were reprinted, usually revised, in *The Dispossessed,* and "Song from 'Cleopatra,'" "The Apparition," "Meditation," "Sanctuary," "The Trial," "Night and the City," "Nineteen Thirty-Eight," "The Curse," and "Ceremony and Vision," which were not reprinted.

The concerns of "Letter to His Brother" are largely the concerns of these twenty poems. They are the poems of a poet living precariously

through a time when "Night now was ever upon the world-city,"[16] and
the imagery of darkness and night dominates most of them. The world
is occasionally seen as a doomed and darkened house, as in the extra-
ordinary last line of "The Curse":[17]

> Only the idiot and the dead
> Stand by, while who were young before
> Wage insolent and guilty war
> By night within that ancient house,
> Immense, black, damned, anonymous.

Or as one already fallen into ruin:[18]

> The oxen gone, the house is fallen where
> Our sons stood, and the wine is spilt, and skew
> Among the broken walls the servants are. . . .

The figure of the poet begins to emerge in these poems. In "Letter to
His Brother," the poet is merely a voice; in some other poems, however,
he has become a visionary figure who can see when those around him
are blinded. This is an early hint, in quite conventional terms, of the
powerful, suffering poet figure of Berryman's later poems. As in "Letter
to His Brother," love is allied with the poet's work—they are both de-
fenses against the dark environment. In "Sanctuary" love provides a
"sanctuary eye among the blind"; in "Meditation" it teaches the poet's
eye "a singular discipline."[19]

Love is not, however, a simple panacea in these poems. While it is,
as in Freud's later work (with which Berryman was well acquainted),
placed over against the forces of aggression and destruction, the two
forces "seldom—perhaps never—appear in isolation from each other, but
are alloyed with each other in varying and very different proportions. . . ."[20]
Thus, even the potentially redemptive force of love can be destructive.
While unalloyed aggression brings destruction to the twilit house of the
world, it mixes with love in "Desires of Men and Women" to bring the
same results on an individual basis. Although the men and women of
this poem "conjure a mansion," stately and civilized, this merely hides
the[21]

> half-lit and lascivious apartments
> That are in fact your goal, for which you'd do
> Murder if you had not your cowardice
> To prop the law. . . .

The potential destructiveness of this most necessary and admirable quality will become of great importance in Berryman's later work. But in that work he will realize that this violence is a part of his own love. Here the poet remains aloof from the men and women of the poem, as if he didn't share this problem with them.

In general, as in "Letter to His Brother," the political threat figures in most of these poems. Yet the only purely political poem in the selection, "Nineteen Thirty-Eight," is one of the weakest. Berryman falls into what Allen Tate called "the tone of pronouncement and prophecy":[22]

> Terror accumulated in September
> Until the island Dove divided up
> A southern ally for the Eagle's feast,
> And trembled as the Eagle fed, knowing
> The gratitude of appetite.
> . . . .
> The winter sky is fatal wings. What voice
> Will spare the aged and the dying year?
> His blood is on all thresholds, bodies found
> Swollen in swollen rivers point their fingers:
> Criminal, to stand as warning.

The Auden influence in this case is debilitating. The rhetoric is swollen and unconvincing. To use Berryman's words from another context, there is no movement "from the earth into mythology,"[23] as there is in, say, "Letter to His Brother."

In the years following the 1940 publication, Berryman wrote more poems that were purely political. In 1941 he published, in *New Directions,* "Five Political Poems": "River Rouge, 1933," "Thanksgiving: Detroit," "The Dangerous Year," "1 September, 1939," and "Communist." Of these poems Jarrell said in an accurate review that they "have lots of Yeats, lots of general politics, a 1939 reissue of *1938,* and a parody of Lord Randall—'Communist' that—but nothing can make me believe that Mr. Berryman wrote this himself, and is not just shielding someone."[24] Life in Detroit and work for the *Nation* are probably more important influences on these poems than Auden, but this doesn't make them any more convincing.

Berryman reprinted the five in his 1942 *Poems,* which was one of Laughlin's "Poet of the Month" series. Dedicated to Bhain Campbell, the volume of eleven poems was "an arbitrary brief selection from work done during 1939 and 1940."[25] The selection included, in addition to the five political poems, "The Moon, The Night and The Men," "A Poem for Bhain," "The Statue" (reprinted from 1940), "At Chinese Checkers," "A Point of Age," and an "Epilogue" about Bhain Campbell's death. The sense of loss occasioned by this death is not merely the loss of a friend, but of a fellow-poet:[26]

> heretics, we converse
> Alert and alone as over a lake of fire
>
> Two white birds following their profession
> Of flight, together fly, loom, fall and rise,
> Certain of the nature and station of their mission.

The idea of the poet-hero is more fully developed in these poems than in Berryman's earlier work. Berryman is beginning here to establish the company of poets—always isolated, always rejected by their culture—with which he was to ally himself for the rest of his career.

Another poet-hero of the volume is Delmore Schwartz, alone and ignored, in "At Chinese Checkers":[27]

> Deep in the unfriendly city Delmore lies
> And cannot sleep, and cannot bring his mind
> And cannot bring those marvellous faculties
> To bear upon the day sunk down behind,
> The unsteady night, or the time to come.

These are the sprouting seeds of *Homage to Mistress Bradstreet.* The poet, rejected by all but fellow poets, is forced by a hostile environment to the edge of madness. And if the images of night and city are still conventional, Berryman's personal involvement is new. Delmore Schwartz is, like Bhain Campbell, the figure of the alienated poet, but he is also Berryman's friend—the lament is both general and personal.

Another important element in the makeup of Berryman's poet figure is introduced in "At Chinese Checkers," and that is the idea that the poet writes out of a sense of loss. Here the loss of childhood is the motivating factor, childhood and "the innocence of love . . . / Virgin with trust" that went with it:[28]

> The gold is lost. But issued from the tomb,
> Delmore's magical tongue.

The loss of childhood is an important factor in much of Berryman's work, and is explicitly related to his father's suicide in later poems. "That mad drive wiped out my childhood," Henry will say much later. The loss of childhood is, conventionally, a loss of innocence, as it is here, but it is also—and more importantly—the loss of trust, the loss of a sense of being cared for, an awareness of aloneness which becomes metaphysical in *The Dream Songs.* On the other side of this coin, having a child entails a responsibility to keep that trust, as Berryman's father did not.

The other long poem in the volume, "A Point of Age," is devoted to a third poet-hero, Berryman himself. "A Point of Age" is a poetic packing of bags in preparation for moving on: "Twenty-five is a time to move away." The season—as in much of Berryman's other work, from "Trophy" onward—is winter; the time is night:[29]

> What then to praise, what love, what look to have?
> The animals who lightless live, alone
> And dark die. We await the rising moon.
> When the moon lifts, a late winter moon,
> Its white face over time where the sun shone
> Gold once, we have a work to do, a grave
> At last for the honourable and exhausted man.

The poet, having suffered the loss of the golden sun (in 1948 Berryman made the pun explicit: "Late on the perilous wood the son flies low"), looks bleakly toward future work. So many of these poems look forward because they reflect the uncertainty of the period and the fears that soon there will be nothing to look forward to—that the civilization will continue to decline, taking the long slide into extinction. The image of the forest, a Dantesque wood, appears here as well as in many of the earlier poems, and is the scene of much of *The Dispossessed.*

But if "A Point of Age" has a conventional tone and resembles much of Berryman's earlier work, it also represents a slight departure from that work. In those poems Berryman had presented us with an intelligent, somewhat despairing, but always impersonal sensibility—little more than a disembodied voice. Here, and in "At Chinese Checkers," the poet is beginning to confront his personal history directly. These are poems about the development of an American poetic sensibility, a sensibility facing a world characterized not only by a moral darkness, but also by loss. In *The Dispossessed* poems like these alternate with poems on the war, giving us a picture of the growth of the poet at a time and in a country "inimical to poetry, gregarious, and impatient of dignity."[30] Berryman had found his subject matter. These were to be his concerns for the rest of his life. What he had not found, as a reading of these poems makes clear, was a manner sufficiently his own. That was to come.

In 1948 Berryman published his first large book, *The Dispossessed,* which he dedicated to his mother. He had previously published most of the poems he now collected, and he collected most of what he had published. The headnote states that "with exceptions for a thematic reason, affecting Section One, the poems stand in what was roughly their order of writing."[31] But this is a bit misleading. There are, in fact, quite a few exceptions, and not all of them are in section 1. The arrangement follows the chronology of the poet's life more accurately than it does the chronology of his writings. Thus, "A Point of Age" comes well before "Letter to His Brother," which is placed shortly before "At Chinese Checkers." The poet begins by saying farewell to youth in section 1. In subsequent sections he moves to England, returns, marries, and, as the environment becomes progressively less stable, ends up, in "A Winter-Piece to a Friend Away," in an asylum, thinking of "the immortal risks our sort run." Alternating with these personal poems are the social poems, which, beginning with "Winter Landscape" and ending with "The Dispossessed," describe the growing madness in the poet's environment. Collected in this way, the poems are more impressive than they would be taken singly. They point toward an overriding concern—the depiction of a pathological epoch of civilization. They point toward "the fateful question" posed at the end of *Civilization and Its Discontents,* a book which often provides a useful gloss on these poems:[32]

The fateful question for the human species seems to me to be whether and to what extent their cultural development will succeed in mastering the disturbance of their communal life by the human instinct of aggression and self-destruction. It may be that in this respect precisely the present time deserves a special interest. Men have gained control over the forces of nature to such an extent that with their help they would have no difficulty in exterminating one another to the last man. They know this, and hence comes a large part of their current unrest, their unhappiness and their mood of anxiety.

Of course, by 1948 this anxiety had had the chance to increase a hundredfold. In "The Dispossessed" this "disturbance of their communal life by the human instinct of aggression" becomes a grotesque melodrama in which aggression wins and "The race is done."

The dispossessed of the poem are, of course, ourselves, suffering from the onset of what Berryman called "bad conscience":[33]

"It was done for us"—your modern intellectual is astonishingly fatalistic. This is the view generally taken, with a gain in uneasiness, of the use of the atomic bomb. . . . The trouble is the future: what they—or what *They* for them—are going to be doing in the months and years and days to come. This is the trouble. In order to be reconciled to *this,* one would have to learn to be reconciled beforehand to an atrocious crime one might well soon commit without having the slightest wish to commit it; and that, I suppose is out of the question. So that men who can think and are moral must stand ready night and day to the orders of blind evil. What has created this is an usurpation of the individual decision, which yet leaves the individual nominally free—and of course actually free if he happens to be a hero.

Thus, we must accept the moral responsibility for an evil that we seemingly had no part in creating. Like the six characters in the Pirandello play, "the Italian page" from which the first line and the "Leading Man," "Juvenile Lead" terminology come from, our parts have been taken over by actors—"It was done for us." The result is "something that . . . is theirs—no longer ours." The volume as a whole follows the course of this dispossession, ending, with "The Dispossessed," in the bombings of Hiroshima and Nagasaki:[34]

> That which a captain and a weaponeer
> one day and one more day did, we did, *ach*
> we did not, *They* did . . . cam slid, the great lock
>
> lodged, and no soul of us all was near was near,—
> an evil sky (where the umbrella bloomed)
> twirled its mustaches, hissed, the ingenue fumed,
>
> poor virgin, and no hero rides. The race
> is done. Drifts through, between the cold black trunks,
> the peachblow glory of the perishing sun
>
> in empty houses where old things take place.

So by the end of the volume not only "the idiot and the dead" but all of us

> Stand by, while who were young before
> Wage insolent and guilty war
> By night within that ancient house,
> Immense, black, damned, anonymous.

The last lines of "The Dispossessed" answer the hope expressed earlier in "Boston Common" that the individual would become a hero, and thus become "actually free," presiding over an era of peace, in which the most violent acts would be fishing or gardening. In "Boston Common" the function of "Jack," the "casual man," would be[35]

> Watching who labour O that all may see
> And savour the blooming world, flower and sound
> Tending and tending to peace . . .

In "The Dispossessed," of course, that hope is shattered—what "blooms" is the umbrella of the atomic bomb, "and no hero rides. The race / is done."

Berryman is very aware in these poems of the relations between the individual life and the process of civilization. "If civilization," Freud wrote,[36]

is a necessary course of development from the family to humanity as a whole, then—as a result of the inborn conflict arising from ambivalence, of the eternal struggle between the trends of love and death—there is inextricably bound up with it an increase of the sense of guilt, which will perhaps reach heights that the individual finds hard to tolerate.

"All wars are civil," Berryman wrote in "Rock-Study with Wanderer." The disruptions of the outer world produce their analogues in the inner landscape. Thus, "The Return," first published in 1938, returns early on in *The Dispossessed* as "The Possessed." If we are dispossessed by the forces of evil, we are also possessed by them; the increasing darkness of the outer world brings on a personal twilight characterized by guilt:[37]

> This afternoon, discomfortable dead
> Drift into doorways, lounge, across the bridge,
> Whittling memory at the water's edge,
> And watch. This is what you inherited.
>
> . . . .
>
> Think on your sins with all intensity.
> The men are on the stair, they will not wait.
> There is a paper-knife to penetrate
> Heart & guilt together. Do it quickly.

"This is what you inherited." In the most personal terms, that inheritance is the loss felt after his father's suicide. But to equate the "discomfortable dead" with Berryman's father is to misread the poem. They are, rather, the objectification of the monstrous aspects of the poet's mind as he lives at those "heights that the individual finds hard to tolerate." He is like the "Imaginary Jew" of Berryman's 1945 story, bearing "in the fading night our general guilt."[38] The poet is a representative man, but in a sense in which Emerson never used the term. He embodies not our potential for wholeness and transcendence, but our potential for suffering and disjunction.

Nevertheless, the poet's personal inheritance begins with the acute sense of loss and guilt occasioned by his father's suicide. The two poems that introduce this theme, "The Ball Poem" and "Fare Well," are placed at the end of section 1, and, having been written later than the rest of the poems in the group, are part of the "exceptions for thematic reasons" affecting the order in that section. "The Ball Poem" is about "the epistemology of loss" and the difficult necessity that it imposes. The boy who lost his ball in the harbor[39]

> is learning, well behind his desperate eyes,
> The epistemology of loss, how to stand up
> Knowing what every man must one day know
> And most know many days, how to stand up. . . .

In this poem Berryman made the discovery[40]

that a commitment of identity can be "reserved," so to speak, with an ambiguous pronoun. The poet himself is both left out and put in; the boy does and does not become him, and we are confronted with a process which is at once a process of life and a process of art. . . . Without this invention . . . I could not have written either of the two long poems that constitute the bulk of my work so far.

The idea of the ambiguous pronoun is important to Berryman's work, but because Berryman called attention to its use here, the poem has had to bear more weight than it can carry. It is probably the most anthologized of Berryman's early poems, for example, but it is a weak representative of his early work. The loss of a ball is a poor objective correlative for the feelings engendered by the loss of a father, and so the "ultimate shaking grief" rings false. Berryman was aware of this difficulty, surely. The problem is making the reader aware of both the importance and the unimportance of this loss—it is only a ball, but as a result of its loss, the child crosses the border from the security of childhood to the insecurity of adulthood. Berryman attempts to distance himself in the beginning of the poem through the mock-nursery rhyme tone—"What, what is he to do?" and the repetition of "merrily"—but the manipulation of tone is unsuccessful, both because he is making fun of the boy rather than the object of his emotion and because we are forced to jump too quickly from the mockery of the first few lines to the "ultimate shaking grief." Compared to Ransom's "Janet Waking," the *locus classicus* of this type of poem, "The Ball Poem" is a failure.

But compared to "Fare Well," which follows it in the volume, "The Ball Poem's" understatement is noticeable. The season of "Fare Well" is winter, and here the spiritual desolation of that season is specifically associated with Berryman's father's suicide. "Fare Well" is as emotional as "The Ball Poem" is restrained:[41]

> Father I fought for Mother, sleep where you sleep!
> I slip into a snowbed with no hurt
> Where warm will be warm enough to part
> Us. As I sink, I weep.

The torture and the lamentations of "Fare Well," although no doubt very real, sometimes seem ironic when read immediately after "The Ball Poem":

> People will take balls,
> Balls will be lost always, little boy,
> And no one buys a ball back.

> What has been taken away should not have been shown,
> I complain, torturing, and then withdrawn.

Part of the problem with "Fare Well" is that there is no ambiguous pronoun, that the commitment of identity is not reserved. Despite the implied Freudianism of "Father I fought for Mother," the poem is stuck in specifics and cannot leap into myth.

This theme of personal desperation continues through the volume, getting more intense as the social environment deteriorates. The poet figure of "A Point of Age" and "At Chinese Checkers" becomes, by the last section of the book, the *poète maudit* of "A Winter-Piece to a Friend Away." The season is again, obviously, winter, the time when "all roads are lost." The poet has vainly fought against "the breaking blizzard's eddies" for years, but has finally reached a dead end, "the massive sorrow of the mental hospital." As he writes to his friend:[42]

> Immortal risks our sort run, to a house
> Reported in a wood ... mould upon bread
> And brain, breath giving out,
> From farms we go by, barking, and shaken head,
> The shrunk pears hang, Hölderlin's weathercock
> Rattles to tireless wind, the fireless landscape rock,
> Artists insane and dead
> Strike like a clock. ...

The wood is the personal analogue of the wood of "Winter Landscape" and the wood that "seeded and towered suddenly" in "The Dispossessed," as well as all of the other woods of the earlier poems. Similarly, the house is a personalized version of the houses of the world of the early poems, from the "Immense, black, damned, anonymous" house of "The Curse" to the "empty house where old things take place" of "The Dispossessed." The outer madness of the social poems and the inner madness of the personal poems come together here. But the poem is not totally despairing, for friendship and sympathy are present: "The thaw alone delays,— / Your letter came!"

Sympathy and love provide the refuge for the poet from the divisive, destructive forces of the world around him. The aspects of life that Berryman admires the most, and finds the most hope in, both here and in his later poems, are love and work. When the antagonist of "The Lovers," another Berryman story, is asked what concerns him the most, he answers, "'Work!—a wife, and work!'" Ironically, the man in the story has no wife—the woman he loves is the mother of the boy narrator. The poet in *The Dispossessed,* however, does have a wife, and he turns to her, especially in the later poems, for refuge:[43]

> Obstinate, gleams from the black world the gay and fair,
> My love loves chocolate, she loves also me,
> And the lightning dances, but I cannot despair.

The family, indeed, is of great significance in Berryman's work. The world of "The Dispossessed" is, among other things, one in which "Rarely a child sings now." It is a phrase that Berryman had used earlier in "The Song of the Young Hawaiian," one of the "Nervous Songs." In both poems it points to the fact that "We are a dying race." The phrase "Rarely a child sings now" seems a bit sentimental, and it is perhaps surprising that Berryman would use it twice, but it emphasizes the importance of the family. A culture which is not having children or caring for its children is doomed. Children in Berryman's work are always potentially redemptive—not so much because they are innocent or trail clouds of glory but because they provide a core of love and responsibility. In "The Nervous Songs" this theme is present, although only in embryo.

"The Nervous Songs" were probably inspired by Rilke's *Die Stimmen,* which are nine songs sung by victims, grotesques: "The Song of the Beggar," "The Song of the Blindman," Drinker, Suicide, Idiot, etc. There are nine "Nervous Songs" as well, but Berryman's grotesques are victims of a declining civilization, and their greatest problems are not physical deformities or injuries (although two, the tortured girl and the captain, have been physically injured in the war) but mental and emotional instabilities. They are remarkably uneven poems. "The Professor's Song" is witty and technically dexterous. "The Captain's Song" is sentimental, verging on the bathetic. The captain leaves "wife & child" to fly a bomber. (Embracing the war means rejecting the family). He is shot down and loses a leg. He remembers warming his wife's feet with his own and wonders, "Will I warm her with one?" "The Song of the Tortured Girl" is frankly bathetic:

> Often, "Nothing worse now can come to us"
> I thought, the winter the young men stayed away,
> My uncle died, and mother broke her crutch.

There is nothing in the poem that indicates that we are to take this any other way but seriously.

The young Hawaiian is unaware of his mental debility. He suffers from a form of pride that is both cause and symptom of a declining civilization: "I swim / Farther than the others, for I swim alone." His refusal to take a mate, to take his responsibilities to the culture seriously, brings about his downfall—he is "smashed to pieces" by Nangganangga, a Hawaiian god Berryman discussed much later in his career, in an essay on another poem about not marrying:[44]

Primitive societies take a dim view of not marrying. Hawaiian mythology, for instance, describes a god called Nangganangga, whose job it is to stand with an immense club on the Road to Paradise and smash off it, into nothingness, any unmarried male who, having died, tries to get by. This way of thinking is precisely Eliot's.

Commitment to the family is one of the most important themes in Berryman's later work. Both Mistress Bradstreet and Henry find their solace in it. Berryman adopted Freud's pair of cultural virtues for strong personal reasons—Berryman's father, after all, deserted his family, and as Henry says, contemplating his own suicide, "the wounds to the survivors is the worst of / the Act."

The emphasis on work in Berryman's poetry is a bit more difficult to understand. The young boy narrator of "The Lovers" is confused by the strange man's reply of "a wife and work!" especially the second term: "I did not understand the words in their starkness—'work' particularly fell into my mind like a word unknown, with its special weight from the idiom of workers in science and art—I did not understand them. . . ."[45] Work, however, like love, performs a harmonious, integrative function, both for the individual and for the community. "No other technique for the conduct of life," Freud wrote,[46] attaches the individual so firmly to reality as laying emphasis on work; for his work at least gives him a secure place in a portion of reality, in the human community. The possibility it offers of displacing a large amount of libidinal components, whether narcissistic, aggressive or even erotic, on to professional work and on the human relations connected with it lends it a value by no means second to what it enjoys as something indispensable to the preservation and justification of existence in society.

This, then, is at least part of the appeal of work to Berryman—it provides a positive, integrative outlet for the aggressive impulses which, if unchecked, may result in a rule of blind evil as in the war. Perhaps equally important, though, is the type of work involved here, for despite all of the risks the poet runs, he is still "at work upon salvation," and his art is a bastion against the forces of a hostile world.

The social theme of the volume, which ends with "The Dispossessed," is introduced in "Winter Landscape," which introduces the volume. In his prefatory note Berryman insisted that "the subject of 'Winter Landscape' is not really the painting by the elder Breughel to which from start to finish the poem refers."[47] He elaborated on this some years later:[48]

Very briefly, the poem's extreme sobriety would seem to represent a reaction, first, against Yeats's gorgeous and seductive rhetoric, and, second, against the hysterical political atmosphere of the period. . . . So far as I can make out, it is a war-poem, of an unusual negative kind. The common title of the picture is "Hunters in the Snow" and of course the poet knows this. But he pretends not to, and calls their spears (twice) "poles," the governing resultant emotion being a certain stubborn incredulity—as the hunters are loosed while the peaceful nations plunge again into war. This is not the subject of Breughel's painting at all, and the interpretation of *the event of the poem* proves that the picture has merely provided necessary material, from a tranquil world, for what is necessary to be said—but which the poet refuses to say—about a violent world.

This interpretation has been disputed. William Martz, for example, has written that "'Winter Landscape' . . . transcribes skillfully from the Breughel painting 'Hunters in the Snow,' but does not realize a meaningful theme about it or, as Berryman intended, about something else."[49] Yet, closely examined, the poem does seem to justify both Berryman's interpretation and its place at the beginning of *The Dispossessed.*

"Winter Landscape" consists of one sentence split into two main clauses of approximately equal length. The transcription from the painting is limited almost completely to prepositional phrases and subordinate clauses within the sentence. Stripped of most of these, the sentence reads:

The three men coming down the winter hill are not aware that in the sandy time to come, the evil waste of history outstretched, they will be seen upon the brow of that same hill: when all their company will have been irrecoverably lost, these men will say what place, what time, what morning occasion sent them into the wood, thence to return as now we see them.

The main clauses of the sentence thus lead us to the question Berryman intended us to ask: "What place, what time, what morning occasion sent them into the wood?" The answer is found in the subordinate clauses which refer to those things "which the poet refuses to say"—namely, the spears and the violence and death that they connote. The emphasis on the men returning—it is going to happen again—and the pun on "morning occasion" reinforce this. Here, as in "Desires of Men and Women," the substratum of an apparently civilized landscape is violent and destructive. During the course of the book Berryman brings us through that landscape to what lies beneath. Note also that "Winter Landscape" introduces the images of woods and winter, which Berryman used almost obsessively and which become increasingly grotesque as the volume progresses, ending in the surrealistic wood of "The Dispossessed" with its "cold black trunks" and "the peachblow glory of the perishing sun." "Winter Landscape" is a quiet, understated poem, but it provides a fitting introduction to a book that ends with the near-hysteria of the title poem.

When *The Dispossessed* was published in 1948, several reviews, although generally favorable, noted a weakening emphasis on style. Repeated is Randall Jarrell's comment, "Doing things in a style all its own sometimes seems the primary object of the poem, and its subject gets a rather spasmodic and fragmentary treatment."[50] What Jarrell was noting (and predicting good things from) was the "new style" of the poems in sections 4 and 5. Indeed, turning the page from "Boston Common" to "Canto Amor" is something of a shock. One moves from

> Helpless under the great crotch lay this man
> Huddled against woe, I had heard defeat
> All day . . .

to

>   yet I may You bless
> always for hér, in fear & joy for hér
> whose gesture summons ever when I grieve
> me back and is my mage and minister.

These last poems with their abrupt juxtapositions and radical inversions of syntax are generally thought to point toward the style of *Homage to Mistress Bradstreet,* in which the voice of the mature Berryman is first heard. Yet it seems quite clear that Berryman had already found the essential aspects of his mature voice in these poems. Of course, with the advantage of hindsight one can see that Berryman's career had pointed toward this style from the beginning. One can find it as early as the last sentence of this section of "Ars Poetica" (1935):

> I stumble strangely over my name
> In the level of speech.
> Use and time should teach
> A fluency of step: came
> Nor comes the sound within my reach.

Technique fascinated Berryman, and he experimented throughout his career, continually developing, and building on what had gone before. Berryman had experimented with radical inversions of syntax not only in his student work but later on: "Prediction if I make, I violate / The just expectancy of youth." Most of the time, however, this emerging style was hidden behind the conventional thirties tone that Berryman used for so long—it is only in the last two sections of *The Dispossessed* that Berryman relies on it heavily. The style is occasionally no more than quirky and eccentric—the use of ampersands, for example, which Berryman persisted in for the rest of his career, does little more than give the appearance of something new—but it is a very flexible technique at its best, capable of remarkably disparate effects. It can be used, as in the preceding quotation from "Letter to His Brother," to impart a formality and stateliness reminiscent of Milton (whom Berryman called "the supreme English master of syntax.")[51] Or it can be used for purely lyric purposes, to enhance the sound, as in "Canto Amor," in a manner reminiscent of Hopkins.

The shift of style evident in these poems is at least partially the result of a hiatus of several years. From 1944 to the winter of 1947, Berryman published almost no verse. Most of the poems in the last two sections of *The Dispossessed* were published in 1948. This allowed Berryman a great deal of time to develop. If we are looking for major watersheds in Berryman's verse, we should most likely look to his years in Cambridge and his reading of Yeats in 1937 and 1938, and to the work which seems to have been done during his hiatus of 1944–47. *The Dispossessed* is of course a great deal more than a record of the early development of the author of *Homage to Mistress Bradstreet* and *The Dream Songs,* but it is that also. By 1948 Berryman had all the technical tools necessary for both his long poems. He had even used the three six-line stanzas of *The Dream Songs* (with a different metrical pattern) in "The Nervous Songs," three of which were the only poems he published between 1944 and 1947. There is one more probable cause for the development during this period. Sometime in 1947 (probably) Berryman wrote 115 sonnets, most of them, like the later work, "crumpling a syntax at a sudden need."

2

BERRYMAN'S SONNETS

Berryman's Sonnets, although not published until 1967, was apparently written during the summer of 1947, while Berryman was a lecturer and fellow in creative writing at Princeton. It is difficult, at this point, to date the composition of the *Sonnets* with absolute certitude. Most references in the poems to events which can be dated point to 1947. The events described in sonnet 20, for example—the awarding of honorary degrees to Truman, Eisenhower, and others—occurred on 18 June 1947. It is likely that the last four sonnets were written later, probably as Berryman was revising the poems for publication. William Meredith has noted that in those sonnets, unlike the earlier ones, Berryman capitalized at the beginning of a line only when it was grammatically necessary.[1] There is some other internal evidence to support this theory. One of the things Berryman did when he revised the poems for publication was to substitute a false name for his mistress's real one. He said in an interview, "I'd used her name a lot, and it was very difficult, because sometimes there were rhymes. So I had to change her name to a name that would rhyme."[2] It is likely, though, that he in fact changed her name to one that would only half-rhyme. The pseudonym "Lise" was probably suggested by the *Diary* of Anne Frank. A line from the book is alluded to in sonnet 113. Anne Frank spelled the name "Lies," pronounced "Leez," and that is the pronunciation used in the last four sonnets. Nowhere else in the volume, though, does the name rhyme with "ease"; it is used as a rhyme word only four times in the earlier sonnets, but each time it rhymes with a word with a short *i* sound, like "this." (At all times in the *Sonnets* the word has only one syllable). This is not conclusive evidence, but it is strongly suggestive. If it is in fact true, then the sequence was originally intended to end with sonnet 111, the implications of which I shall briefly discuss later.

Presumably, the potentially scandalous nature of the affair the poems describe was responsible for the twenty-year delay in publication, although Berryman's divorce in 1956 and his substitution of "Lise" for his mistress's real name would have minimized any possible scandal long before 1967. There were probably several reasons for the delay, among them, perhaps, commercial ones. The reason Berryman seized on in a dream song preface to the volume was, oddly enough, the "confessional" nature of the poems:

> He made, a thousand years ago, a-many songs
> for an Excellent lady, wif whom he was in wuv,
> shall now he publish them?
> Has he the right, upon that old young man,
> to bare his nervous system
> & display all the clouds again as they were above?
>
> As a friend of the Court I would say, let them die.
> What does anything matter? Burn them up,
> put them in a bank vault.
> I thought of that and when I returned to this country
> I took them out again. The original fault
> will not be undone by fire.
>
> The original fault was whether wickedness
> was soluble in art. History says it is,
> Jacques Maritain says it is,
> barely. So free them to the winds that play,
> let boys & girls with these old songs have holiday
> if they feel like it.

This may, finally, have been the most important reason for the delay: that the sequence remains too personal or, rather, as we shall see, too limited to be considered a major work.

The poems are generally regarded as the minor work of a poet who went on to do more important things, a bridge between Berryman the promising talent and Berryman the major poet. Entertaining, but not to be taken too seriously. "The speaker's epithet for himself," writes William Martz, "is 'The adulter and bizarre of thirty-two' (105), but the sonnets hardly make us feel much about his guilt. What they do make us feel is his energy, his humor, and his exuberance."[3] Similarly, Robert Mazzocco wrote in a review of the *Sonnets* that "you cannot take Berryman too seriously as a lover."[4] But this attitude is a bit misleading. Although the

Sonnets is a minor work, and although it is frequently exuberant and witty, it is also deadly serious: "The original fault was whether wickedness / was soluble in art." Berryman is often a comic lover, but that comic stance masks a painful reality.

The occasion for the *Sonnets* is an affair between the poet and a blonde woman whom he calls Lise. Both are married. The setting is Princeton and environs, and the year 1947 (during Princeton's "bicentennial of an affair with truth . . . / Not turned out well" [sonnet 20]). Their love, consummated very early on, progresses through the summer and is ended by Lise as the fall begins. During most of the sequence the poet and Lise are separated: Lise is either at the shore on vacation or has left Berryman waiting vainly at their trysting place. Although they manage to make love occasionally, most of the sequence consists of Berryman considering the affair they have fallen into. Like most sonnet sequences, these are very lonely poems.

The sonnets, modelled on the Elizabethan sequence, are Petrarchan in form—the octaves usually rhyme *abba abba,* while the sestets ring various changes on the *cde cde* rhyme scheme. The sonnet sequence is an excellent way of turning a personal experience into art—a different and potentially more valuable method for Berryman than the Yeatsian meditative-descriptive form he had frequently used in the past. It was not unusual for Berryman to turn to a Renaissance form; his interest in the literature of the English Renaissance was both long and intense. He was an Oldham Shakespeare Scholar at Cambridge in 1938, was working on a critical edition of *King Lear* around the time these poems were written, and published an edition of Nashe's *Unfortunate Traveller* in 1960. The choice of the sonnet sequence form was a clear break from Yeats and a move toward finding his own form—a step backward in order to take two steps forward.

The sequence that *Berryman's Sonnets* resembles most closely is Sidney's *Astrophel and Stella.* Berryman's subject, like Sidney's, is the poet's passion for his lady; like Sidney's, Berryman's focus is on the psychological and moral ramifications of that passion. The differences between the two, however, are many. Unlike Sidney's, *Berryman's Sonnets* is frankly autobiographical; it does not hide an affair, it reveals one. The main character is named Berryman. Berryman is married, Astrophel is not. Astrophel affects to be an amateur poet, writing only out of love; Berryman is a professional, worried about the effect the affair might have on his verse. The most important difference, however, is that in Berryman's sequence the poet has already consummated that which Astrophel only devoutly wished. The moral and psychological problems facing the two protagonists are thus quite different. Astrophel works out the consequences of an act which he does not, finally, engage in. The problems he considers are conditional and abstract. Berryman must face the consequences of an act which he is in the process of committing. His problems are thus immediate and existential.

Berryman's Lise, "blonde, barefoot, beautiful," appears at times to be a conventional heroine for a sonnet sequence, offering the poet inspiration and a vision of ideal beauty and love, whose "shining . . . rays my room with gold" (sonnet 2). At other times, however, she seems, like the age in which she lives, "inimical to poetry, gregarious, and impatient of dignity." More interested in Bach than in Berryman, a heavier drinker than the poet, Lise is often more Dark Lady than Stella or Laura, offering the poet only lust, keeping him from his work and making him a hypocrite and moral leper:

> . . I am this strange thing I despised; you are.
> To become ourselves we are these wayward things.
> And the lies at noon, months' tremblings, who foresaw?
> And I did not foresee fraud of the Law
> The scarecrow restraining like a man, its rings
> Blank . . my love's eyes familiar as a scar!
> [sonnet 45]

One can, as Robert Mazzocco has done, explain this paradoxically alternating view as poor characterization: "Unfortunately, Lise is little more than a vaguely theatrical presence, nubile and distracting, mysteriously and alternately Petrarch's Laura, Anne Frank, the daughter of a Texas oilman, a matron in an institution, and 'strip-murderer.' Lise is also blonde, 'more clear / and witching than your sister Venus.' "[5] Part of the reason for this alternating view, of course, is the nature of the subject. While love can be ennobling and inspiring, it can also, by allowing passion to rule over reason, be degrading. This commonplace of Elizabethan sequences is also true of *Berryman's Sonnets:*

> And does the old wound shudder open? Shall
> I nurse again my days to a girl's sight,
> Feeling the bandaged and unquiet night
> Slide? Writhe in silly ecstasy? Banal
> Greetings rehearse till a quotidian drawl
> Carols a promise? Stoop an acolyte
> Who stood my master? [sonnet 39]

More important for understanding this attitude, though, is the adulterous nature of the affair. Their love, even when beautiful, is contrary to the laws of the civilization. Indeed, "fraud of the Law" is the central moral dilemma of the *Sonnets.* Berryman, for all his complexity, is, like the modern poet he describes in *The Arts of Reading,* "on the side of the Turks—primitive qualities, loyalty, survival, simple things."[6] The phrases run through his work: "a wife and work," "Loyalty and Art," "husbandship and crafting." The violation of these principles by giving in to lust is not taken lightly: "My God, this isn't what I *want!*" (sonnet 104). He has described bachelorhood as "the sameness and triviality that are the lot of one who never succeeded in adopting his human responsibilities at all."[7] In "The Song of the Young Hawaiian," one of the "Nervous Songs," as we have seen, he portrayed the arrogant young bachelor "Whom Nangganangga smashed to pieces on / The road to Paradise,"[8] for bachelors, irresponsible during their lives, are not allowed the rewards of heaven. The family, after all, is the foundation of the civilization, and adultery is a betrayal of the family.

Berryman is also afraid, in the *Sonnets,* that the second of his goals —his work, which is equally important to the culture—will be harmed by his affair:

> But I lie still,
> Strengthless and smiling under a maenad rule.
> Whose limbs worked once, whose imagination's grail
> Many or some would nourish, must now I fill
> My strength with desire, my cup with your tongue,
> no more Melpomene's, but Erato's fool? [sonnet 4]

To surrender thus to passion, Berryman fears, is to give up service to the muse of tragedy in order to serve the lesser muse of love verse. By betraying his "proper work" he is again avoiding his responsibility to the culture, to those whom his "imagination's grail / . . . would nourish." He is, in short, violating the two basic principles of community, love and work.

The law Berryman and Lise are breaking is continually and painfully present in the figures of the husband and wife they are deceiving. Lise's husband, unlike the deceived husband of most sonnet sequences, is not a fool in possession of a priceless gem. He is, rather, a "kind and good man; with a gun; hunts hope" (sonnet 21), while Berryman is "lawless, empty, without rights" (sonnet 19). Berryman's wife is "sandy-haired mild good and most beautiful / Most helpless and devoted" (sonnet 69), while Berryman is "adulter and bizarre of thirty-two" (sonnet 105). There is thus no possible excuse for their behavior. There is also little joy or exuberance in their deception:

Audacities and fêtes of the drunken weeks!
One step false pitches all down . . come and pour
Another . . Strange, warningless we four
Locked, crocked together, two of us made sneaks—
Who can't get at each other—midnights of freaks
On crepitant surfaces, a kiss blind from the door . .
One head suspects, drooping and vaguely sore,
Something entirely sad, skew, she not seeks . .

"You'll give me ulcers if all this keeps up"
You moaned . . One only, ignorant and kind,
Saves his own life useful and usual,
Blind to the witch-antinomy I sup
Spinning between the laws on the black edge, blind
Head—O do I?—I dance to disannul.   [sonnet 33]

The poet, drunk and out of control, is not merely a sneak who has hurt
his wife—he has allied himself with the side of disruption rather than
integration: "I dance to disannul." But sonnet 34 continues the thoughts
of sonnet 33:

"I *couldn't leave* you" you confessed next day.
Our law too binds. Grossly however bound
And jacketed apart, ensample-wound,
We come so little and can so little stay
Together, what can we know? Anything may
Amaze me: this did. Ah, to work underground
Slowly and wholly in your vein profound . .

"Our law too binds"—binds also and binds too strongly. Thus Berryman's
"witch-antinomy," spinning between the laws of the civilization and the
needs of the self. On the one hand, stability and responsibility, and on
the other, passion and knowledge. In Freudian terms, Berryman is caught
between libidinal needs and the superego. Between

A spot of poontang on a five-foot piece,
Diminutive, but room *enough* . . like clay
To finger eager on some torrid day . .
Who'd throw her black hair back, and hang and tease
                    [sonnet 104]

and

                    ghosts crowd, dense,
Down in the dark shop bare stems with their Should

Not! Should not sleepwalks where no clocks agree! [sonnet 3]

According to Freud, of course, this is the human condition. But it is not simply a matter of libidinal compulsion in conflict with the laws of the culture. Their affair also offers a real vision of love, "deafening rumors of / The complete conversations of the angels" (sonnet 2). The antinomy is real, the choices are equal: "Our law too binds." It is on this irony that the sequence hinges: "To become ourselves we are these wayward things."

Their passion is often, as in sonnet 33, associated with drunkenness—both are forms of irresponsibility, both evidence of a loss of control, both associated with the "maenad rule." (Berryman makes a similar point in prose, in his *Stephen Crane*. In discussing "The Blue Hotel" he mentions "the Swede, crazy, drunk—two stages of irresponsibility. . . .")[9] Another traditional image associated with their passion is the ocean or a ship lost in a storm. Sonnet 15 is a version of "My Galley Chargèd With Forgetfulness," in which Berryman once again emphasizes his twin goals by changing Wyatt's

> The stars be hid that led me to this pain,
> Drowned in reason that should me comfort,
> And I remain despairing of the port.

to

> Muffled in capes of waves my clear sighs, torn,
> Hitherto most clear,—Loyalty and Art.
> And I begin now to despair of port.

Sonnet 25 is also constructed around the image of a ship lost in "the foam / Irresponsible." Elsewhere their passion is portrayed as waves, or the uncontrollable tide. In sonnet 80 Berryman imagines them on a beach, on the edge between land and sea, a part of neither. In the first sonnet, before the affair is properly begun, lack of water and a mirage provide the central images:

> But who not flanks the wells of uncanny light
> Sudden in bright sand towering? A bone sunned white.
> Considering travellers bypass these and parch.

And in one of the last sonnets Berryman punningly concludes that "he should have stuck to his own mate / Before he went a-coming across the sea-O" (sonnet 107).

Occasionally Berryman wishes for a resolution to the conflict, for a calm life, both literally and metaphorically sober:

> still I hope
> Sometime to dine with you, sometime to go
> Sober to bed, a proper citizen.   [sonnet 93]

But such conflicts as his are more a way of life than an accident of it, and in his more rational moments the poet realizes that there is no easy way out of his situation—to be sober is to give up too much:

> Sensible, coarse, and moral; in decent brown;
> Its money doling to an orphanage;
> Sober . . well-spirited but sober; sage
> Plain nourishing life nor you nor I could down
> I doubt, our blinkers lost, blood like a clown
> Dancing upon a one-night hot-foot stage,
> Brains in a high wind, high brains . . .   [sonnet 58]

The possessor of such a sober life is a neuter, doling its money out. And while Berryman occasionally wishes for *that,* too ("Unman me" [sonnet 105]), brains, vision, and blood militate against such a solution. So the sequence alternates between the obligations to one side and to the other. And so Berryman's attitude toward the affair and Lise alternates throughout the sequence, as he stands in the middle, "spinning between the laws, on the black edge."

Berryman's Sonnets is thus as much an exploration of the poet's consciousness as it is the record of a love affair. In a central sonnet Berryman aptly compares himself to the man on the Penal Colony's machine:

> Demand me again what Kafka's riddles mean,
> For I am the penal colony's prime scribe:
> From solitary, firing against the tribe
> Uncanny judgments ancient and unclean.
> I am the officer flat on my own machine,
> Priest of the one Law no despair can bribe,
> On whom the mort-prongs hover to inscribe
> "I FELL IN LOVE," . . O none of this foreseen,
> Adulteries and divorces cold I judged
> And strapped the tramps flat. Now the harrow trembles
> Down, a strap snaps, I wave—out of control—
> To you to change the legend has not budged
> These years: make the machine grave on me (stumbles
> Someone to latch the strap) "I MET MY SOUL."   [sonnet 73]

Thus, Lise is, the affair is, a vehicle for self-knowledge, a way for the poet, almost against his will, to see himself. Lise directs the poet's gaze, not toward a far-removed ideal beauty, but inward, toward a more painful and unpleasant vision. In a very different way from Astrophel, Berryman looks in his heart and writes.

For this reason Berryman's fears of becoming "Erato's fool," of not fulfilling his responsibilities as a poet, are unfounded. His verse is not primarily love verse. There are very few seduction pieces here. Rather, the *Sonnets* deals, as Berryman said of Pound's love verse, with "certain themes in the life of the modern poet: indecision-decision and infidelity-fidelity."[10] They are part of Berryman's continual bout with Loyalty and Art, and as such attempt to deal with the poet's total sensibility. As Berryman says in a sonnet about the *Sonnets:*

> you
> Jitterbug more than you pavanne, poor dears . .
> Only you seem to want to hunt the whole
> House through, scrutators of the difficult soul
> Native here—and pomp's not for pioneers.   [sonnet 87]

I don't think, as we shall see, that the *Sonnets* do "hunt the whole / House through," but they do explore rooms that had previously remained closed. In this regard, the *Sonnets* represents a breakthrough for Berryman. He had never before used such intimate material in his verse. The subject of the *Sonnets* is not very different from the subject of "Desires of Men and Women," but Berryman has travelled a long way from the rather modish sneering of the earlier poem. The[11]

> half-lit and lascivious apartments
> That are in fact your goal, for which you'd do
> Murder if you had not your cowardice
> To prop the law . . .

are now the dark rooms of the poet's own sensibility.

Thus, if one were looking for Berryman's "confessional verse," the *Sonnets* would be the place to start. It is clearly unreasonable to assume, as M. L. Rosenthal seems to do,[12] that Berryman entered the post-*Life Studies* "confessional movement" with *77 Dream Songs* in 1964. On the contrary—throughout his career, from the earliest Yeats imitations on, Berryman experimented with various ways of turning personal experience into art. At the same time he was constantly aware of the need for his poems to "leap into myth," to move out from the personal to the general. And in the *Sonnets,* which is one of Berryman's most personal works, there is a similar attempt to "leap into myth." The original problem, as he makes clear in the preface, was not the affair, but the more general problem of "whether wickedness was soluble in art." In the *Sonnets* he attempted, through adopting an old convention, to put his specific and particular character in a general situation—to portray, as he portrays in his other work, the life of the representative man, the modern poet who bears the burdens of his culture.

Nevertheless, *Berryman's Sonnets* cannot be said to be a completely successful attempt, precisely because these poems do *not* "hunt the whole / House through," at least not very convincingly. When Berryman restricts himself, as he does in most of the *Sonnets,* to "fidelity-infidelity" and the ramifications of that theme, mostly Freudian, in the culture, the poems are generally effective. But Berryman is not success-ful—as he is in his later work—in expanding this central theme to include broader considerations. Sonnets which attempt to relate his particular situation to political or metaphysical themes are generally flat and un-convincing. This is not because the form of the sonnet sequence is not flexible enough to handle a variety of themes—it is—but because Berry-man was discovering themes that he didn't yet know how to handle.

One important aspect of Berryman's mature sensibility, for example, is that it is profoundly divided—he both believes in and doubts the existence of a Christian God. He is aware of centuries of metaphysical thought, but cannot quite come to an understanding of the relation of that thought to his own pains and pleasures. Now, the Berryman of the *Sonnets* is divided in many ways, as we have seen, but this most impor-tant split of the later Berryman is present here only in embryo, and his doubts are very weakly expressed:

> Nothing there? nothing up in the sky alive,
> Invisibly considering? . . I wonder.
> Sometimes I heard Him in traditional thunder;
> Sometimes in sweet rain, or in a great 'plane, I've
> Concluded that I heard Him not. You thrive
> So, where I pine. See no adjustment blunder?
> Job was alone with Satan? Job? [sonnet 35]

Compare this with the same doubts expressed in *Homage to Mistress Bradstreet:*[13]

> God awaits us (but I am yielding) who Hell wars.

> —I cannot feel myself God waits. He flies
> nearer a kindly world; or he is flown.
> One Saturday's rescue

> won't show. Man is entirely alone
> may be. I am a man of griefs & fits
> trying to be my friend.

Part of the reason for the success of the passage from *Homage to Mistress Bradstreet* is that Berryman makes us feel the torment of unbelief instead of keeping things at an abstract and "literary" level as he does with the mention of Job in the passage from the *Sonnets*. The passage from *Mistress Bradstreet,* on the other hand, very effectively directs our attention to the poet himself: "I am a man of griefs & fits." Berryman goes on in the sestet of sonnet 35 to describe hearing, one morning, the voice of God forgiving him, with the implication that things would certainly be better if such a thing happened, but nothing further is done with this in the sequence. The problem of belief is clearly bothering Berryman, but he cannot yet utilize this problem effectively in his poetry. One also gets the impression that Berryman is uncomfortable with the word "sin"—he is more comfortable with its analogue "fraud of the Law." As a result, the speculations about God in the *Sonnets* just lie there, largely obscured by the Freudianism. In *Mistress Bradstreet* Berryman solves this problem by projecting his belief onto Anne Bradstreet, and speaking about sin through her lips. Translated into historical terms, the affair with Lise can, in *Mistress Bradstreet,* take on historical and metaphysical overtones that seem out of place in the *Sonnets.*

If, as I think most likely and have suggested earlier, the sequence originally ended with sonnet 111, then the metaphysical aspect of the poems returns at the conclusion, and the *Sonnets* ends in the same way that *Homage to Mistress Bradstreet* and *The Dream Songs* do—with submission after a long period of rebellion. Once again, though, the references to God are not adequately prepared for.

The *Sonnets* points toward future work in other ways as well; at times, indeed, almost too presciently:

> Burnt cork, my leer, my Groucho crouch and rush,
> No more my nature than Cyrano's: we
> Are "hindered characters" and mock the time. . . .
> [sonnet 100]

It is possible that this, too, was added when Berryman revised the *Sonnets* for publication. I doubt it—I think it is probably just a coincidental pointer toward future work—but there is no way, at this point, to prove it. This raises a potentially more serious problem, however—the possibility that Berryman radically revised the *Sonnets* stylistically, imposing on them the style of his mature work. However, I think that this is unlikely. Berryman was not an obsessive reviser in the manner of, say, Auden. The revisions made in the poems published in *The Dispossessed* are, by and large, relatively minor. Furthermore, the style of the *Sonnets* is also present in "The Nervous Songs," three of which were published in 1946. Moreover, although one cannot trust everything that Berryman said about his work, he claimed that he did not revise the poems extensively.[14] I think it is safe to say, then, that the affair with Lise provided Berryman with, among a great many other things, the opportunity to practice his art and experiment with rhyme schemes, rhetorical conventions, and most of all syntax.

One influence on Berryman's style which I have not mentioned thus far, but which seems to figure here, is the work of Tristan Corbière. Berryman mentioned Corbière (with Rilke and Lorca) as one of the passions of "those remote days" in an interview published in 1965, and it is most probable that those days coincided with the composition of the *Sonnets*. One of the sonnets (109) is about Corbière's odd relationship with Armida-Josefina Cuchiani and her lover Count Rodolphe Battine, and quotes a phrase from René Martineau's biography of the poet. The sonnet quite accurately describes the relationship, but doesn't mention that after the count took his mistress to Paris, Corbière wrote "Le Poète Contumace." Berryman, in a similar situation, is writing the *Sonnets*. There, I would say with Berryman, "the resemblance ends."

There are, however, some indications in the sequence of the influence of Corbière's style on Berryman's. Berryman's description of himself in sonnet 53, for example, "*Ermite-amateur* in the midst of boobs," is taken from Corbière's description of himself in "Le Poète Contumace": "Un ermite-amateur, chassé par la rafale."[15] Minor aspects of Corbière's work, such as the use of dashes and ellipses in the place of more traditional punctuation marks, also seem to have influenced the *Sonnets*. More important, though, I think, is the more general liberating influence of Corbière's work in its distortions of syntax and in its emphasis on the internal effects of alliteration and internal rhyme:[16]

—Moi, j'en suis degoûté;—
Dans me degoûts surtout, j'ai des goûts élégants. . . .

It is quite likely that this kind of word play opened up for Berryman the possibilities of lines like "The *mots* fly, and the flies mope on the food," in sonnet 53. It is difficult to describe with any accuracy the extent of Corbière's influence. I think it likely that it was stronger than

Hopkins's—the mixture of high and low diction in Corbière's work is
a clear precedent for Berryman's mature style. In any event, the features
of that mature style—the omission of function-words, the mixture of
diction, the separation of subject and verb, of verb and object, and
the other syntactic shuffling of the later poems—are all present in these
poems.

When this technique works, it is very effective. Take, for example,
the portrayal of Berryman's wife's confused pain at one of their parties:

> One head suspects, drooping and vaguely sore,
> Something entirely sad, skew, she not seeks. . . .
>
> [sonnet 33]

The grammar gradually loses hold as the painful words linked by the
alliteration build up. The spondee in the last foot of the second line
emphasizes the meaning and the iamb-trochee of the third and fourth
feet make the rhythm of the line as "skew" as the grammar. Indeed,
the free metrical substitution in this line gives the effect of springing
the rhythm within a regular metrical pattern. This, as we shall see, is
also typical of the metric of *Homage to Mistress Bradstreet.*

Even when Berryman's style obscures the meaning, it can be suc-
cessful:

> What can to you this music wakes my years
> (I work you here a wistful specimen)
> Be, to you affable and supple, when
> The music they call music fills your ears?

Even here it is not the long hesitation before the verb that causes the
trouble, but "wakes my years," where too many function words have
been left out. The general meaning is quite clear, and the music provided
by the internal rhymes and the gentle alliteration more than balances
the slight confusion.

The *Sonnets* provided practice in other areas as well. It was after all,
a sequence of more or less independent, introspective poems strung on
a narrative line, recording at the same time external and internal events.
They also combined Berryman's favorite stanza lengths—eight lines and
six lines. He was experimenting with six-line stanzas at about the same
time in "The Nervous Songs" and *The Black Book,* but that form was
to lie fallow for a few years. He was shortly to return to experimenting
with the eight-line stanza, which had long been his favorite, in another,
more celebrated love poem.

3

HOMAGE TO MISTRESS BRADSTREET

The period following the writing of the *Sonnets* was an especially
busy one for Berryman. Most of the poems of *His Thought Made Pock-
ets and the Plane Buckt* were written and published between 1948 and
1953. *The Dispossessed* appeared in 1948, *Stephen Crane* in 1950. But
in the background all this time was a poem about Anne Bradstreet begun
in the late forties and then abandoned with only a stanza and a half writ-
ten. When Berryman returned to it in the early fifties (after a great deal
of research), he found that what he had planned as a seven- or eight-
stanza poem was going to be a great deal longer. When he finished it
(with the aid of a Guggenheim Fellowship in 1951-52), *Homage to
Mistress Bradstreet* had fifty-seven stanzas and was slightly longer than
The Waste Land. Although it appeared, in full, in the *Partisan Review*
in September 1953, it was not published in book form until 1956. The
publisher to whom it was optioned (presumably William Sloane, who
had published *The Dispossessed*) rejected it, and it was not until Robert
Giroux, a long-time friend of Berryman's who was convinced that the
poem was a masterpiece, became editor-in-chief at Farrar, Straus and
Cudahy, that the poem appeared.[1]

Homage to Mistress Bradstreet is in many ways Berryman's central
work, the breakthrough that fulfills earlier promises of genius and makes
new promises for the future. This is true of both the language of the
poem and its thematic elements. In *Mistress Bradstreet* Berryman brought
together several concerns that he had touched on in his earlier work
and which would be of increasing importance in his later work: loss,
rebellion and submission, the importance of the family. He also brought
up, through the voice of Mistress Bradstreet, that difficult word which

he had mentioned briefly and to no apparent purpose in the *Sonnets,* but which he would use frequently in later works: God. *Mistress Bradstreet* is an ambitious poem, but it attempts less than *The Dream Songs* and, because it is more coherent, is more successful. But it was a long time a-bornin'.

Berryman's five-year writer's block was broken by several things, as Berryman explained in his *Paris Review* interview,[2] but the most important element to the poem was the idea of tempting Anne Bradstreet, and not merely tempting her, but tempting her with himself. The "adulter and bizarre," no longer thirty-two, projected onto history the affair recorded in, but not completely exorcised by, the *Sonnets.* Thus, Mistress Bradstreet repeats Lise's words, including the emphatically wavering *"want"*: "I *want* to take you for my lover." And, similarly, Berryman repeats to Mistress Bradstreet his reply to Lise: "Do."[3] It is tempting to say that *Homage to Mistress Bradstreet* is *Berryman's Sonnets* writ large, but this would be a bit misleading. Let us say, rather, that in the *Sonnets* Berryman discovered an important theme, adultery, which was closely related to his major thematic concern, the relation between the poet and his culture, but—perhaps because he was too close to the actual experience—Berryman didn't quite know what to do with it. *Berryman's Sonnets* is an attempt to generalize his experience but, finally, not a successful one. Berryman was unable to include everything he wanted to say. What he needed was a form that would allow both the lyric voice of the sonnet sequence and the scope in subject matter of the epic. What he needed, indeed, is what every ambitious poet since Wordsworth has needed—a form that doesn't exist. *Homage to Mistress Bradstreet* and *The Dream Songs* are Berryman's two attempts to create a narrative form that would include both history and the personal voice. In *Homage to Mistress Bradstreet* he faced the problem of form by yoking two forms together and creating what might be called a love poem containing history, a poem in which the muse and heroine are one, a "sourcing" which Berryman quite literally invokes in the beginning, calling her toward him:

> Out of maize & air
> your body's made, and moves. I summon, see,
> from the centuries it.   [3.1–3]

But Berryman's choice of muse and heroine seems unusual. Anne Bradstreet is hardly a major poet; indeed, she is seldom even a good one. One would not expect an innovative twentieth-century poet to be interested in "this boring high-minded Puritan woman."[4] Born Anne

Dudley in England in 1612, she married Simon Bradstreet when she was sixteen, shortly after a bout with smallpox. Two years later they crossed the Atlantic on the *Arbella,* settling first at Ipswich and later at North Andover. She bore the first of her eight children in 1633, three years after her arrival in the New World. In 1650 her poems were published without her knowledge in London under the title *The Tenth Muse Lately Sprung up in America.* Sylvester and Quarles were, as Berryman notes, "her favorite poets; unfortunately."[5] She died in 1672. Her only claim to Berryman's interest would seem to be that she was the first American poet, and thus the stuff that myths are made of. But Berryman, unlike Hart Crane, whose *Bridge* has often been compared to *Mistress Bradstreet,* is not primarily concerned with creating American myth. *Mistress Bradstreet* is concerned with more particular relations—relations between individuals and between individuals and society.

It is a commonplace by now that for this reason the poem is about the woman, not the poetess, and not the historical woman either, exactly, but the historical woman distorted for thematic reasons. Unlike the historical Anne Bradstreet, the Mistress Bradstreet of the poem is disfigured by her smallpox, has an insensitive husband and a trying marriage, knows Anne Hutchinson.[6] She is self-conscious and full of doubt. She is not the "boring high-minded Puritan woman" who wrote the *Quaternions,* but is, rather, the woman who wrote, "I have often been perplexed that I have not found that constant joy in my pilgrimage and refreshing which I supposed most of the servants of God have."[7]

This is all quite true. Nevertheless, the Anne Bradstreet of the poem *is* a poetess, and, despite Berryman's remarks to the contrary,[8] it is important to remember this. Her work conflicts with her life and contributes to her dissatisfactions—"Ambition mines, atrocious, in" (15.8). Early in the poem she uses her verse to hide from the unpleasant pioneer environment—"Versing, I shroud among the dynasties" (12.1). Near the end of the poem, after she has chosen the life over the work, she contrasts her poems unfavorably with her children. Her children "loft, how their sizes delight and grate." The poems, on the other hand, are "proportioned, spiritless" (42).

Moreover, although both she and the poet denigrate her verse, several of the most striking lines in the poem are either direct quotations from, or echoes of, her work: "at which my heart rose, but I did submit" (7. 8, from "To My Dear Children"); "Strangers & pilgrims fare we here, / declaring we seek a City" (8.4–5, from "Meditation 53"); "Motes that hop in sunlight" (9.6, from "Another Letter to Her Husband"); "at fourteen / I found my heart more carnal and sitting loose from God" (13.7–8, from "To My Dear Children"); "and holiness on horses' bells shall stand" (51.5, from "A Dialogue Between Old England and New"); "sinkings and droopings" (51.8, from "To My Dear Children"). These lines offer tacit tribute to her work as well as reinforce a sense of verisimilitude.

This love poem containing history must balance between two modes, the narrative and the lyric, but must lean toward the narrative. "When I finally woke up to the fact that I was involved in a long poem," Berryman wrote, "one of my first thoughts was: Narrative! let's have narrative, and at least one dominant personality."[9] The stanza form of the poem had to be capable of handling narrative flow as well as lyric effects. The form he finally settled on was the result of a great deal of experimentation with stanza forms, especially six-line and eight-line stanzas. The *Sonnets* had, of course, given him a great deal of practice in writing these stanzas, but in the *Sonnets* he had been basically restricted to pentameter lines. He had from very early in his career preferred a mixture of line lengths in a stanza—a preference he no doubt received from his reading of Yeats, who had frequently mixed four-beat and five-beat lines in his stanzas. Poems like "Fare Well" and "The Long Home," published at about the time Berryman was beginning *Homage,* are indications of this experimentation. The former is in eight-line stanzas, the fourth and eighth lines of which are three-beat, the rest five-beat. The latter is in six-line stanzas, 5-4-5-4-5-3, rhyming from the inside out (the third and fourth lines rhyming, the second and fifth and the first and sixth).

Another result of this experimentation was an abortive long poem, begun at about the same time as *Homage, The Black Book.* Four sections of the poem were published in *Poetry* in 1950, two of which were reprinted along with a third, previously unpublished, in *His Thought Made Pockets and the Plane Buckt. The Black Book* was to have been a poem about the Nazi atrocities in Poland, the title coming from a survey of the Jews killed in Poland, *The Black Book of Poland.*[10] The material was too painful for him to deal with, however, and the project was abandoned.

The bits of the poem that have been published are painful indeed, dealing with individual atrocities—rape and murder, the consciousness of a man about to be gassed, and similar subjects. Each section of the poem is formal, but each is written in a different form. The four sections published in *Poetry* are written in stanzas of nine, eight, six, and four lines respectively. With the exception of the last section, which is written in traditional quatrains, each of the sections uses a different combination of line lengths. The first section, for example, entitled "not him" in *Poetry,* uses a variation of the Spenserian stanza with one

two-beat and two four-beat lines in addition to the final alexandrine.
The second section ("2") consists of eight-line stanzas, with the follow-
ing beat-pattern: 5-5-4-4-5-4-3-6. The third section ("the will") is written
in the dream song stanza, 5-5-3-5-5-3, and is the earliest example of
Berryman's use of the dream song form.

The form that he decided upon for *Homage* most closely resembles
that of the second section of *The Black Book,* and it is well suited for
a mixture of narrative and lyric. The feet are usually 5-5-3-4-5-5-3-6, and
the rhyme scheme is a less schematic version of the inside-out rhyme
scheme of "The Long Home"—lines 1 and 8 always rhyme, lines 5 and
6 usually rhyme, and the other lines rhyme variously. Berryman wanted
a form "at once flexible and grave, intense and quiet, able to deal with
matter both high and low,"[11] and he obviously succeeded. Its mixture
of short and long lines allows for a variety of effects, and its final alex-
andrine provides a sense of dignity and formality. Each stanza is self-
contained, but run-on stanzas are frequently used in narrative sections
of the poem, and do not seem awkward.

But if a stanza form can help a narrative, it cannot create it, and
although Berryman was aware of the importance of narrative, there are
times when his stylistic quirks, his by now natural inclinations to play
with the language, seem to interfere with the simple necessity of telling
a story. For example, in the fifth stanza, when Mistress Bradstreet is
describing the voyage to the New World, we are told this:

> bone-sad cold, sleet, scurvy; so were ill
> many as one day we could have no sermons. . . .

There seems to be no point to the awkward inversion, "so were ill / many."
It stops the action when Berryman needs to move it forward. It is not
even done—poetaster's scourge—for the rhyme. The only difference be-
tween the phrase as it stands and "so many / were ill one day . . ."
seems to be one of clarity.

But this is not usually the case. Berryman generally walks quite stead-
ily on the line between lyric intensity and narrative drive. Take, for ex-
ample, the beginning of stanza 9:

> Winter than summer worse, that first, like a file
> on a quick . . .

To change this to

> That first winter worse than summer, like a file
> on a quick . . .

would be to lose both beauty and motion to dullness. The trochees of my version give the effect of starting each foot with a heave. Similarly, my version makes a botch of Berryman's very effective alliteration and internal rhyme.

Once one is familiar with the syntactic shifts and omission of function words typical of Berryman's style, it is hard to believe that the possibilities of expression it has opened up were not there all the time. While there are stylistic failures in the poem, like "so were ill / Many," and borderline phrases like "Can be hope a cloak" (40.8), most of the time the language is its own justification. It is capable of remarkably disparate effects:

> Drydust in God's eye the aquavivid skin
> of Simon snoring lit with fountaining dawn
> when my eyes unlid, sad.   [15.1-3]

> When by me in the dusk my child sits down
> I am myself.   [42.1-2]

In both these quotations the rhythm combines with the language to produce the effect. In the first the irregular metrical pattern reinforces the emotional pain of the passage; in the second the regular iambs support the comfortable feeling of the words. The inversions are both appropriate and effective. A more normal sentence order in the second quotation, for example, would make it much less interesting:

> When my child sits down beside me in the dusk . . .

Berryman reserves the meat of both the clause and the sentence by inverting the order.

One should not get the impression, however, that the poem is a series of inversions. As Virginia Prescott Clark has pointed out in "The Syntax of John Berryman's *Homage to Mistress Bradstreet*," "the aspect of the syntax of *Homage to Mistress Bradstreet* that has been least noticed (or at least not commented on) is the extensive amount of simplicity in the poem."[12] As Mrs. Clark has noted, most of the sentences in the poem are simple sentences, and most of the syntactic variations are made within that structure. The relatively few deviations are so striking, however, that they give the impression that the entire poem deviates from normal sentence patterns.

What adds to this impression is the rhythm of the poem. In his review of *Mistress Bradstreet* John Ciardi wrote that "Berryman's one unquestioned mastery is of rhythm, a rhythm so intensely compacted and forward moving as to be a communication in itself."[13] There *is* a mastery of rhythm exhibited in the poem, but the rhythm is not one in which, as Mr. Ciardi put it, "there are relatively few unaccented syllables." The basic metrical pattern of the poem, as a glance at the first stanza will show, is iambic, and although Berryman substitutes quite freely at times, he never deserts the iamb or the trochee for so long that we lose our metrical expectations. As one would expect, Berryman substitutes most freely in those passages of the highest emotional intensity. The driving effects of these passages, what Ciardi called "forward moving" rhythm, are accomplished by the use of relatively more unaccented syllables than the iambic pattern allows. Stanza 20, describing the birth of Anne's first child, is a good example:

> hide me | forev|er I work | thrust I | must free
>
> now I | all mus|cles & | bones con|centrate
>
> what is | living | from dying?
>
> Simon | I must | leave you | so un|tidy
>
> Monster | you are | killing | me Be | sure
>
> I'll have | you la|ter Wom|en do | endure
>
> I can | *can* no | longer
>
> and it pas|ses the wret|ched trap | whelming | and I | am me . . .

Substitutions in the first two lines make them difficult to scan. There are too many different kinds of feet here for one to get any real sense of regularity. But the pattern is not as irregular as it seems—elide the "er" of "forever" in the first line and we have a fairly normal iambic line with two trochaic substitutions:

> hide me | forever | I work | thrust I | must free

One can say that the extra syllable springs the rhythm, but it is simpler to say that there is an anapestic substitution in the important third foot.

In any case, the first two lines do buffet the reader about: the anapest and the iamb-trochee combinations, which give the effect of triple rhythm, drive the lines forward, while the spondee and the anapest-trochee combination halt the forward motion. The rhythm quite accu-rately portrays Mistress Bradstreet's emotional state. But Berryman does not allow this rhythmic buffeting to go on for very long. The stanza settles into a regular metrical pattern until the last line, where anapestic substitutions drive the line into the triumphantly iambic "and I am me." Without the rhythmic regularity, the rhythmically deviant lines would lose their effect, and the passage would become heavily accented prose; without the deviant lines there would be no sense of resolution in the iambs at the end of the stanza. As with the syntactic deviations, how-ever, the rhythmic deviations are so noticeable that one tends to over-look the regularities.

The poem is highly organized. It is divided into three sections and has an exordium and a coda of four stanzas each. The first section, a monologue by Anne which runs from stanza 5 to 25.2, is concerned with her life up to the birth of her first child. The second section (25.3-39.3) is a dialogue between the poet and Anne. The third section (39.4-53) treats her later life and her death. "The poem," Berryman wrote, "laid itself out in a series of rebellions. I had her rebel first against the new environment and above all against her barrenness (which in fact lasted for years), then against her marriage (which in fact seems to have been brilliantly happy), and finally against her continuing life of illness, loss, and age."[14]

The first part of the first section describes the landing of the *Arbella* and the harshness of the new environment: heat and starvation the first summer, wolves and cold the first winter. The hardships and deaths of the first months are an early cause of dissatisfaction:

> How long with nothing in the ruinous heat,
> clams & acorns stomaching, distinction perishing,
> at which my heart rose,
> with brackish water, we would sing.
> When whispers knew the Governor's last bread
> was browning in his oven, we were discourag'd.
> The Lady Arbella dying—
> dyings—at which my heart rose, but I did submit. [8]

The phrase "at which my heart rose" does not mean "made me happy," as several critics have assumed. It is used in the sense in which Mistress Bradstreet used it: "I . . . came into this country, where I found a new world and new manners, at which my heart rose. But after I was con-vinced it was the way of God, I submitted to it. . . ."[15] She is made happy neither by Lady Arbella's death nor by "distinction perishing." The pattern of rebellion and submission is thus established very early on.

The hostility of the physical environment is not the only cause of Mistress Bradstreet's pain. As the new society grows stronger, it grows more repressive:

> I remember who
> in meeting smiled & was punisht, and I know who
> whispered & was stockt.
> We lead a thoughtful life. [16]

The gentle irony of "We lead a thoughtful life" grows as the poem progresses. By stanza 24, just before Anne's dialogue with the poet, her irony has become sarcasm: "Forswearing it otherwise, they starch their minds." Neither the physical nor the social environments offer Anne any peace or consolation. Her marriage, instead of offering her a haven from this strife, proves to be yet another trial. In the middle of the first section, she speaks of her childhood and her marriage to Simon. After her bout with smallpox, sent to her, she thinks, as a punishment for passion ("For at fourteen / I found my heart more carnal and sitting loose from God"), she had fallen into passion again, this time mistaking it for love:

> That year for my sorry face
> so-much-older Simon burned,
> so Father smiled, with love. Their will be done.
> He to me ill lingeringly, learning to shun
> a bliss, a lightning blood
> vouchsafed, what did seem life. [14]

The syntax of the last three lines is difficult. The sense seems to be, though, that when she was ill and getting accustomed to being unhappy, Simon "vouchsafed" to her passion ("a lightning blood") that, mistakenly, "did seem life." As a result she is, by the following stanza, dissatisfied with her marriage and worried about her sanity: "Women have gone mad / at twenty-one" (15.7-8). She repeats this error of mistaking passion for love yet again, it seems to me, in her tryst with the poet. In both cases she is rescued by her children—the birth of her first child brings love to her marriage, and the "prattle of children" saves her from her illicit love with the poet.

Anne is thus threatened to the point of madness by her marriage, her society, and by her environment. This threat is removed, for the moment at least, by a three-line pregnancy and a three-stanza birth. The moment of the birth of her first child is for Anne both a moment of triumph and an affirmation of the faith which will be further tested during the course of the poem:

> . . . I did it with my body!
> One proud tug greens Heaven. Marvellous,
> unforbidding Majesty.
> Swell, imperious bells. I fly.
> Mountainous, woman not breaks and will bend:
> sways God nearby: anguish comes to an end.   [21]

It is fitting that the poet whose major work ends with the words "my heavy daughter" should present as "the moment of the poem's supreme triumph"[16] the birth of Mistress Bradstreet's first child. It is through this painful, ecstatic bout with and discovery of her body that Anne discovers herself: "I am me / drencht & powerful" (20–21). For the moment, at least, she is fulfilled.

But the moment does not last. Anguish comes to an end, she will learn, only when life comes to an end. Although the specific conflicts in Anne's life change, the state of conflict does not. Her growing sense of herself and her family ("Beloved household" [22]) only increases her awareness of the hypocrisy and repression of her society, against which she rebels, but which she does not reject. The battleground for this struggle remains her own mind, and thus she faces, not the physical exile of Anne Hutchinson, but the mental exile of madness. This struggle reaches a peak when Anne Hutchinson is exiled for "Factioning passion" (24.8). Repulsed by that passion, she falls into another, and her dialogue with the poet begins.

The second section of the poem may be thought of as Anne's bout with loyalty. The sensuality which had enabled her to triumph in the birth scene ("I did it with my body!" [21]) now comes into conflict with her commitment to her family. Lonely and despairing, she explores the possibilities of adultery with the poet in "a sort of extended witch-seductress and demon-lover bit."[17] The poet and Anne are both attracted and repelled by the desire they feel for each other across the centuries. "You must not love me," Anne says, "but I do not bid you cease" (26.8). She finds both delight and fear in the relationship, and her attitude changes from stanza to stanza. Like the Berryman of *Berryman's Sonnets* Anne finds herself in violation of moral law:

> Falls on me what I like a witch,
> for lawless holds, annihilations of law
> which Time and he and man abhor, foresaw . . .   [28]

Unlike Berryman Anne can speak in straightforwardly religious terms; she accepts the God that he doubts. She realizes that the penalty for her violation of the law is damnation: "I fear Hell's hammer-wind" (37), but

at the same time she is both tempted ("but I am yielding") and rebel-
lious ("I throw hostile glances towards God"). The poet feels that "Man
is entirely alone / may be" (35), but nevertheless he fears, if not Hell,
a hellish dream-life:

> I trundle the bodies, on the iron bars,
> over that fire backward & forth; they burn. [34.1-2]

Nevertheless, their passionate selves overcome their fears, and they
touch and kiss. When Anne says to the poet, "Talk to me," he responds
with a marvel of sensuality that Berryman has described as "an only half-
subdued aria-stanza":[18]

> —It is Spring's New England. Pussy willows wedge
> up in the wet. Milky crestings, fringed
> yellow, in heaven, eyed
> by the melting hand-in-hand or mere
> desirers single, heavy-footed, rapt,
> make surge poor human hearts. Venus is trapt—
> the hefty pike shifts, sheer—
> in Orion blazing. [31]

But such innocent-sounding passion has violent undertones. At the end
of the stanza Venus is trapped in Orion. By stanza 37 the ambiguity of
Orion's pike is resolved—it has become "a male great pestle" which
"smashes / small women swarming towards the mortar's rim in vain."
For this reason repression, although rebelled against, is necessary, and
when asked to "Sing a concord of our thought," the poet prays to east-
ern icons to "refrain my western lust." Thus, the moment of the poet's
most intimate contact with Anne is by no means a tender interlude.
Indeed, what they have in common in this section is their highly self-
conscious sense of struggle with themselves.

Anne's struggle is ended by a return to the family:

> Evil dissolves, & love, like foam;
> that love. Prattle of children powers me home,
> my heart claps like the swan's
> under a frenzy of *who* love me & who shine. [39]

It is in her children that she finds herself. Her cry at the moment of
birth—"I am me"—is echoed early in the third section: "When by me
in the dusk my child sits down / I am myself" (42). Indeed, the whole
third section, in which Anne becomes reconciled to the less than perfect

world around her, is dominated by her sense of family and her growing sense of loss as members of her family die: "This our land has ghosted with / our dead: I am home" (44). The losses have their consolations. Anne need no longer say "I am Ruth away" (9); she can now say "I am at home." And although individual members of the family cannot survive, the family itself will endure. There is a victory in submission. And although Anne rebels again at the end of her life—"Hard at the outset; in the ending thus hard, thus?" (46)—this is more the plaint of a stoic than the cry of a rebel. By the time Anne approaches death, she has achieved an acceptance of God's world in all of its usually painful variety, and a realization of His rather limited but nonetheless vital mercy:

> Hangnails, piles, fibs, life's also.
> But we are that from which draws back a thumb.   [50]

She is ready for the final submission:

> Wandering pacemaker, unsteadying friend,
> in a redskin calm I wait:
> beat when you will our end.   [51]

In the second stanza of the prologue, the poet describes Anne's new environment:

> Outside the New World winters in grand dark
> white air lashing high thro' the virgin stands
> foxes down foxholes sigh,
> surely the English heart quails, stunned. . . . [2]

He describes his own environment in the second stanza of the coda:

> Already with the wounded flying
> dark air fills, I am a closet of secrets dying,
> races murder, foxholes hold men,
> reactor piles wage slow upon the wet brain rime.   [55]

Things seem to have gotten worse. The "white air lashing high thro' the virgin stands" of the pioneer environment has become the "dark air" flying with wounded; "foxhole" has become a military term. The poet inhabits the world of "The Dispossessed," threatened by total destruction. But if their worlds are different, their situations are similar: they are both threatened by their environments, their societies, and perhaps most importantly, themselves. The poet is writing to Anne not as one at the end of a decline to one at its beginning, but as a person caught in a similar (and ever-present) trap. He is "a man of griefs and fits / trying to be my friend" (35), looking to Mistress Bradstreet as both kindred spirit and exemplar. Sharing her life and her struggles has enabled him to come to terms with his own. After their brief flirtation with passion is over, he is able to write to Anne at "all your ages":

> O all your ages at the mercy of my loves
> together lie at once, forever or
> so long as I happen.
> In the rain of pain & departure, still
> Love has no body and presides the sun,
> and elfs from silence melody. I run.
> Hover, utter, still,
> a sourcing whom my lost candle like the firefly loves. [57]

The repeated "still" at the end of lines 4 and 7 brings the poem to a quiet close, but one that implies continuity. It also brings us back to the first stanza, which, equally quietly, had begun the poem by repeating "still" as an end-word three times. And the song which we read in the stillness expresses, not the lust of the adulterer, but the innocent, bodiless love represented by the childlike fireflies of stanzas 54 and 57, offering a small and flickering light in the general darkness.

4

THE DREAM SONGS

About a year after the publication of *Homage to Mistress Bradstreet* in 1953, Berryman, "having again taken leave of my wits, or collected them . . . began a second long poem,"[1] the working title of which was *The Dream Songs*. "Once one has succeeded in any degree with a long poem," he wrote, "dread and fascination fight it out to exclude, on the whole, short poems, or so I found out."[2] The term "long poem," however, is an ambiguous one, and can refer to a poem of four hundred lines or to one of four hundred pages. Berryman probably intended his new long poem to be only slightly longer than *Homage to Mistress Bradstreet,* but he ended up with a poem of almost 7,000 lines.

On 6 November 1959 five dream songs appeared in the *Times Literary Supplement.* The five later became numbers 1, 5, 75, 67, and 77 of *77 Dream Songs.* Printed together in *TLS* in 1959, they were, in a sense, a précis of the book that was to follow, and indicate that Berryman had the beginnings and endings of his first volume (and perhaps of the entire poem as it was then conceived) in mind very early on: Huffy Henry, having suffered a loss, is "at odds wif de world & its God." He puts forth a book, performs an operation on himself, and makes ready to move on.

Berryman then proceeded, over the next five years, to fill in the middle of the volume. The same process was repeated when Berryman wrote the rest of *The Dream Songs*—he established the ending and then went on to fill in the middle. He clearly intended to end the poem long before 385—the present song 385 was originally published as "161: The Last Song." What had been begun, then, as a "long poem" of roughly the length of *The Bridge,* had become, as Berryman continued to write, a "long poem" like the *Cantos.* Berryman knew how the poem was going to end (with Henry's discovery, in his daughter, of continuity and love), but that didn't prevent the middle of the poem from growing much longer than he had intended and, as we shall see, radically changing the architectonics of the piece.

As the poem grew and the years wore on, the line between Berryman's poem and Berryman's life became at times a very fine one. At times, indeed, individual songs simply became vehicles for the expression of Berryman's peeves about minor aspects of his life. If Berryman had trouble with the mail, for example, Henry complained about it. Trivial experiences *can* make good poetry, of course, but frequently in *The Dream Songs*—especially in the latter sections of the poem—they do not; they remain records of trivial experiences. There is, it seems to me, no question that this reduction of Henry and his experiences harms the poem. At the same time let me emphasize that this doesn't happen so often that *The Dream Songs* dwindles into the expression of a series of merely personal grumblings. This will be made evident, I think, if we examine the character of Henry.

Berryman was always very coy about the relation between Henry and himself. He wrote in his preface to *The Dream Songs* that the poem is

> essentially about an imaginary character (not the poet, not me) named Henry, a white American in early middle age sometimes in blackface, who has suffered an irreversible loss and talks about himself sometimes in the first person, sometimes in the third, sometimes even in the second; he has a friend, never named, who addresses him as Mr Bones and variants thereof.

Berryman insisted in interviews, moreover, that although Henry was a private nickname for Berryman—for the poet, for "me"—Henry "is nothing but a series of conceptions."[3] In the same interview, however, Berryman, apparently unintentionally, confused himself with his character, calling himself "Henry." Henry *is* Berryman, of course—Berryman's "we touch at certain points" is an understatement—but he is also both more and less than Berryman, and that "more" and "less" are important.

From evidence in the poem it seems quite clear that Henry is intended to be a representative figure. He is yet another of Berryman's poet-heroes, taking "immortal risks" and bearing "in the fading night our general guilt." Berryman's subject is the life of the modern poet, and that subject is not only personal but also national and metaphysical; it is absolutely necessary that Henry be a broad enough character to be able to contain all these concerns. The obvious precedent here is *Song of Myself,* with the important difference that in *The Dream Songs* the poet is united with the rest of us not through a transcendental vision, but through suffering. In song 242, which begins "About that 'me,'" Berryman describes a woman visiting Henry's office and breaking into tears. He cries with her and at the end of the song says "I am her."

Saying this in one song does not make it true for all the songs, of course, but it clearly states Berryman's intention. When this characterization of Henry is successful, we are given a picture of a comic poet-hero, taking upon himself our suffering, and bodying it forth in song, saying, with Jeremiah in Lamentations, "I am their musick." When it does not work, as in "Henry's Mail," mentioned above, we are merely given a picture of Berryman.

Henry is also less than Berryman. In obvious ways, of course: Henry, as Berryman pointed out, doesn't brush his teeth, for example. But also in less obvious and more important ways. For example, Henry is an alcoholic, as was Berryman. Yet, with the exception of a few asides, we never get a realistic, specific picture of Henry's alcoholism. Berryman portrays him as either a comic drunk or a philosophical drunk. The embarrassing, degrading situations that alcoholics almost inevitably get into are missing from the picture. Henry's drinking never leads him to the kind of extremities that the consul in Lowry's *Under the Volcano* faces constantly. The embarrassments, recriminations, and loss of friends that this kind of behavior elicits are omitted from *The Dream Songs*. That they were a part of Berryman's life, we need only turn to *Recovery* to discover, but they are not a part of Henry's life. The reason for this may have been Berryman's unwillingness to face the disturbing aspects of his own character squarely, but the effect of it on the poem is a distancing and generalizing one. Henry becomes a comic type, less a portrait of his author than a caricature of him, bearing roughly the same resemblance to Berryman that W. C. Fields's movie characters bear to Fields.

Henry's name is also important. It is a personal name for Berryman, but it is also a name that Berryman spent pages discussing in his study of Stephen Crane, and the resemblances between Berryman's Henry and Crane's Henrys is—again, despite Berryman's disclaimer—at certain points, striking. Henry Johnson in "The Monster" is a Negro made faceless and driven mad by saving his master's son from a fire, and who is later persecuted by the people of Whilomville for his disfigurement. And Henry Fleming, of course, is the "panic-stricken farm boy"[4] whose fear overcomes his pretensions. This "nexus Negro-War," as Berryman called it, is as much a part of *The Dream Songs* as it is of Crane's work, and is certainly more conscious. For Berryman, "all wars are civil," and Berryman's description of the typical Crane character as "pretentious and scared" is equally applicable to his own Henry.

The Dream Songs is different in form from *Homage to Mistress Brad-street,* but in theme it is similar. In many respects *The Dream Songs* is a longer and more complex treatment of the themes Berryman had explored in the earlier poem. Like Mistress Bradstreet Henry rebels against his environment, his family, himself, and God. Like Mistress Bradstreet Henry ultimately finds in his family the values necessary for survival in and, indeed, triumph over, a hostile world. At the center of Henry's world, though, is an element that figures only peripherally in the earlier poem—loss:

> I can't go into the meaning of the dream
> except to say a sense of total LOSS
> afflicted me thereof:
> an absolute disappearance of continuity & love
> and children away at school, the weight of the cross,
> and everything is what it seems. [101]

This dream accurately describes the world of most of *The Dream Songs.* Henry's project during most of the poem is survival in the face of such an environment. Only in the seventh section is Henry allowed the triumph of discovering (or rediscovering) "continuity & love."

Henry's sense of loss is a figured bass to the songs, always there, the painful foundation of the work. The first loss is familial—Henry's father's suicide provides the pattern for the other losses of the poem:

> Save us from shotguns & fathers' suicides.
> It all depends on who you're the father *of*
> if you want to kill yourself—
> a bad example, murder of oneself. . . . [235]

As Henry says, "It all centered in the end on the suicide / in which I am an expert, deep & wide" (136). Other suicides—Hemingway's, Sylvia Plath's, copies of the original—occur with alarming frequency as the poem progresses. But Henry's father's suicide is itself a part of a larger pattern, at the center of which is the "hidden God," *deus absconditus,* who, by withdrawing from the world, has precipitated the corruption and the pain which now characterize it, in the same way that Henry's father's withdrawal caused Henry's personal pain. For this reason, during much of the poem "God's Henry's enemy" (13). Henry is a reluctant survivor who is "cross with god who has wrecked this generation," although he realizes that "we must submit. / *Later*" (153).

This pattern of losses elicits a paradoxical pattern of emotion in Henry. He is first of all extremely attracted to death himself. Henry is an evader, and death is the ultimate evasion. But while attracted to suicide for this reason, he is for the same reason afraid of it. The ultimate evasion is also the ultimate betrayal, and the one that Henry knows the most about:

> relevant experts
>
> say the wounds to the survivors is
> the worst of the Act, the worst of the Act! Sit still,
> maybe the goblins will go away, leaving you free,
> your breath coming normally. . . .   [345]

Suicide would end Henry's pain and it would fit the pattern. But it would also inflict that pattern upon those who survive him. As Berryman said, "He's very brave, Henry, in that he keeps on living after other people have dropped dead."[5] So the suicide poems in the volume are antisuicide poems, assertions, however tenuous, of responsibility and life over against the death force, which is almost a palpable presence in the book. This is the conflict between the forces of love and death that Berryman had dealt with in even his earliest work, as the often personified forces of destruction, "The evening multitudes of sin / Crowd in upon us all."[6] This conflict is frequently presented in terms of war imagery, as it was in his earlier work. The internal and external wars of *The Dispossessed* are here in the forms of Henry's civil war, "his own warring state," and his fifty-year war with his environment. Henry is heroic in placing himself over against the forces of destruction in himself and his environment; comic in his fear and almost constant desire to avoid that inescapable conflict.

Henry's physical environment is an America in which "the rats / have moved in, mostly, and this is for real" (7). In his political guise Henry Pussy-cat is out to get the rats and, as in song 22, reestablish the spirit of Adams and Jefferson. At this level, the loss of Henry's friends is the loss of his companions in this struggle, who are leaving a crumbling country to the "sur-vivid fools" who survive and contribute to its disintegration, as in "The Lay of Ike" and the "Wake-Song." The political songs in *The Dream Songs* serve much the same purpose as the political poems in *The Dispossessed:* they place the poet in the darkened world-city, and help to emphasize the fact that the problems Henry bears are not just personal, but are the problems of the culture. At the same time, though, despite Henry's claims of patriotism, America never takes the place of importance in *The Dream Songs* that it has in, say, *Song of Myself* or even the *Cantos.* America remains, by and large, "the darkened world," the equivalent of "the city" in Berryman's earlier work. By Book 7 America has become "the country of the dead" (279), which Henry must leave in order to become "not good but better" (350).

To a certain extent, the conditions of the modern world are the cause of much of the despair of *The Dream Songs.* The world of the poem is not very different from the world of "The Dispossessed," in which "no hero rides. The race / is done." This fear that the end of the race is imminent, that we are at the end of a long decline, and that "Man has undertaken the top job of all, / *son fin*" (46), occurs periodically in the poem. It is viewed in relation to the other deaths and losses of the poem, fulfilling the pattern. But if Henry's difficulties are more intense than they would have been in the past, at bottom his problems are not new, nor are they merely the product of twentieth-century life:

> It's miserable how many   miserable are
> over the spread world at this tick of time.
> These mysteries that I'm
> rehearsing in the dark did brighter minds
> much bother through them ages, whom who finds
> guilty for failure?   [223]

As with the case of America, the general is more important than the specific. The problem is less twentieth-century life than it is life itself, the attempt to live right in a world that makes it very difficult:

> After the lightning, this afternoon, came thunder:
> the natural world makes sense: cats hate water
> and love fish.   [233]

As the reviewer of *77 Dream Songs* in *TLS* wrote, Henry yearns for "an ordered but not inhuman stability."[7] In a world where "cats hate water / and love fish," such a desire is difficult to satisfy. Henry is a man frantically seeking harmony and stability in a perversely inharmonious and unstable world. Further, it is tempting to see a double meaning in these lines, pointing to the metaphysical aspects of Henry's problem, which are the concern of many of these songs. Henry, after all, is Henry Pussy-cat, who loves, or would like to love, Christ the fish, and who hates the water which is no longer the water of spiritual initiation ("Thro' a race of water once I went: happiness" [44]), but the "grand sea . . . which will then us toss / & endlessly us undo" (303).

Such a reading may strain the lines; nevertheless, the metaphysical aspects of the poem are important. Christopher Ricks, in an excellent review essay, pointed out the resemblances between *The Dream Songs* and *In Memoriam,* and noted that like all good elegies (*Lycidas* as well as *In Memoriam*), *The Dream Songs* can't but be a theodicy. Berryman's poem, for all its fractures and its fractiousness, is as intensely a theodicy—"a vindication of divine providence in view of the existence of evil"—as *In Memoriam;* as intensely, and as equivocally. "God so loves his creatures when he treats them so?"[8]

If *The Dream Songs* resembles *In Memoriam* in this particular, it also resembles another poem, one to which Berryman draws our attention repeatedly, and one which, more accurately than *In Memoriam,* defines Henry's stance vis-à-vis God—Lamentations. The epigraphs from Lamentations and the references to it in the poem have caused a certain amount of confusion. William Wasserstrom, in an important article written before *The Dream Songs* was completed, found a rather complex structural principle based on Lamentations (no longer valid), and came to this conclusion about the thematic import of the epigraphs: "We infer that the cycle as a whole, for all its hodgepodge of association, is single-minded in pursuit of one theme: Fear not."[9] There are difficulties with this inference, however. Berryman seemed to answer it in the epigraphs to *His Toy, His Dream, His Rest:*

> NO INTERESTING PROJECT CAN BE EMBARKED ON
> WITHOUT FEAR. I SHALL BE SCARED TO DEATH
> HALF THE TIME.
> —Sir Francis Chichester in Sydney
>
> FOR MY PART I AM ALWAYS FRIGHTENED, AND VERY
> MUCH SO. I FEAR THE FUTURE OF ALL ENGAGEMENTS.
> —Gordon in Khartoum

The implications of both the text and the epigraphs seem to be, given the situation, how could one not be "scared to death half the time," as indeed Henry is?

Berryman did not want us to turn from Lamentations with the conclusion that we should "fear not," but I think he did want us to note the many similarities between the worlds of the two poems, and to read *The Dream Songs* in light of the biblical poem. Berryman turned to Jeremiah, as he had earlier turned to Mistress Bradstreet, as "a sourcing." Consider the similarities. Like *The Dream Songs,* Lamentations provides a personal response to a general disaster: "I am their Musick." In Lamentations, as in *The Dream Songs,* the cause of the disaster is the Lord's rejection—he has apparently deserted the people of Zion, the city has been destroyed: "Thou hast utterly rejected us; thou art very wroth against us" (5.22). Lamentations, writes Norman Gottwald, is a substantially modified funeral song, in the early chapters of which "Grief for the fallen is the most powerful single emotion."[10] The Lord is "as an enemy" (2.5) to Jeremiah and the people of Jerusalem. He has "trodden under foot all my mighty men in the midst of me" (1.15). The inhabitants of Jerusalem are "orphans and fatherless. . . . Our fathers have sinned, and are not; and we have borne their iniquities" (5.3, 5.7). Their skin is "black like an oven" (5.10) because of the famine the Lord has visited upon them. God has trapped and enchained the poet: "He hath hedged me about, that I cannot get out; he hath made my chain heavy" (3.7). The poet tries to understand the situation, rebels against it, but realizes that he must ultimately submit. Gottwald writes: "Submission in Lamentations is an admonition, an exemplary standard, and even within the same poem the old cry of vengeance is raised once more."[11] "We must submit," says Henry. "*Later.*" In Lamentations, as in *The Dream Songs,* the poet is the representative sufferer who is nevertheless rejected by his peers: "I was a derision to all my people; and their song all the day" (3.14).

In many of these cases, clearly, Lamentations is not a source for Berryman's poem but a precedent. To take the most obvious example, Berryman did not make Henry fatherless because the people of Jerusalem are fatherless. In some cases, however, Berryman seems to have turned to Lamentations as a source—some of Henry's dream imagery echoes specific images from the earlier poem. Sometimes these echoes are direct, as in "God's Henry's enemy" or "That isna Henry limping. That's a hobble / clapped on mere Henry by the most high GOD ." Usually, though, they are more subtle and distorted. For example, in Lamentations God is described as "a bear lying in wait, and as a lion in secret places" (3.10), and Henry frequently uses these images in his thoughts about God. God portrayed as a big cat is more terrifying than comforting:

> Does the validity of the dream-life suppose a Maker?
> If so what a careless monster he must be, whole,
> taking the claws with the purr.   [317]

Henry Pussy-cat is, one suspects, made in the image of this God. The image of God as a bear is rendered, at times, in a more amusing way:

> But foes I sniff!
> My nose in all directions! I be so brave
> I creep into an Arctic cave
> for the rectal temperature of the biggest bear
> hibernating—in my left hand sugar. [120]

The "biggest bear" here has removed himself from the world by hibernating, and he is, not without reason, associated with the Arctic. Winter is a recurring image in *The Dream Songs,* almost as pervasive as it was in *The Dispossessed,* and for the same reason. Winter for Berryman was the season of loss, of lovelessness, of despair. It is the season that Berryman was both figuratively and literally thrust into after his father's suicide, as the family came north from the Deep South, and it is very frequently the season of *The Dream Songs,* "a final sense of being right out in the cold, / unkissed" (3). God is associated with this cold and with snow, another frequent image in the poem ("Complex his task . . . produces snow" [174]). Henry's father is also associated with bears ("One man, wide / in the mind, and tendoned like a grizzly" [34]), and his loss is associated with the cold:

> a powerful swimmer, to take one of us along
> as company in the defeat sublime,
> freezing my helpless mother. . . .   [145]

The emotional death of winter is like physical death for Henry: he is both attracted to it and repelled by it. In an early dream in which Henry is hunted down like Bogart in *High Sierra,* he slips and falls into the snow. His response to this fall is, "It's golden here in the snow" (9). This is a golden oblivion, but as Henry says in a later song, "It's fool's gold. But I go in for that" (36). Variations of this dream occur several times in the sequence, and indicate a gradual improvement in Henry's situation. In 209 Henry is rebelling against this frozen emptiness:

> Henry lay cold & golden in the snow
> toward whom the universe once more howled "No"—
> once more & again.
> "What pricks have you agin' me,—liquor laws
> the appearance in my house of owls & saws,—
> decanted unto the world of men?"
>
> "Divulge we further: somewhat is because
> you loner, you storm off away without pause
> across the sad ice. . . ."

In later dreams it is not Henry but a female figure, a "high heroine," who lies "cold & golden." Henry has become a rescue figure (as he was in song 68, in which he can perform with Bessie Smith because there is "nobody in the snow on call"). The "high heroine" is most likely an aspect of Henry himself, an emotional and spiritual aspect which was frozen by the death of his father and the loss of his God; she lies in a "wilderness of bears." Henry's task is to rescue this part of himself and bring it back to life:

> Cold & golden lay the high heroine
> in a wilderness of bears. His spirit fled
> upon this apparition.
> She never moved but the bears were moved to move
> and if he could have been sure that she was dead
> he would have fled for all his love
>
> leaving behind him fractured vows, for he loathed bears.
> Their giant forelegs & their terrible paws
> not to mention their teeth, theirs
> Like an old sabre-tooth tiger's famished & wild
> hurling himself upon a mastodon
> and gorging, reconciled.
>
> Just once, the tiger wondered to itself:
> I am their enemy, I have enemies
> almost as bad as Fr. Rolfe;
> friendship is *out*. How then can we administer our affairs
> in the absence of slaves & stewards, if you please,
> who may hire us for theirs?   [291]

Here we have an unusually complete example of Henry's dream imagery and Berryman's associational method, which mingles images from Lamentations and other literary works with images from Henry's earlier dreams. The frigid wilderness is inhabited by a threatening God and father figure in the form of the bears, which stand between Henry and the rescue of the "high heroine." The bears then become, by association, the tiger, and an enemy of man, whose only mode of "reconciliation"— with the mastodon at least—is violence. (This is probably an allusion to "Gerontion": "The tiger springs in the new year. Us he devours.") The tiger, by a similar process of association, becomes the slaveowner, trying to figure out how to administer his affairs. (The reference to "Fr. Rolfe" —"Baron Corvo"—is ambiguous, the "Fr." standing for both "Frederick" and "Father," a reference to Rolfe's unsuccessful attempt to become a priest and his subsequent religious mania. Rolfe is a minor hero in *The Dream Songs:* the type of the outcast Christian.) The song portrays the cruelty, the coldness, and the violence of God the enemy and slaveowner, but also the perplexity: God the tiger is just as confused as man the pussy-cat. Henry, typically, is a mixture of heroism and cowardice: he's *there*, but very reluctantly, and scared to death.

The conflict of these dreams is at least partially resolved near the end of the sequence, in a dream in which the heroine is rescued, but is not yet made whole:

> In so far as repair
> is possible, we'll lie her in the sun
> forever . . .
>
> Until her lover comes: let him be good
> quietly to her, and her blocked faith restore. . . .
>
> Cold & golden lay the high heroine
> in a wilderness of bears. Let one man in.
> One is enough.
> Fish for the master, who will do you well,
> rely not on the stormy citadel—
> it's a matter of love. [372]

The "one man" here is, I suspect, Christ, the master for whom Henry's injured soul must fish. The resolution is only partial because there is no union with Christ, only the admonition to find him. However, the heroine probably reappears as the Dancer in song 382. In that song, which will be discussed in greater detail later, she is "free" and "dances Henry away."

There is a great deal of Christian imagery in *The Dream Songs*, but such imagery is generally used in the negative, as it were: Henry cannot find Christ, he cannot come to terms with the notion of a benevolent God. Despite Berryman's later conversion—or return—to Christianity, *The Dream Songs* is the work, not of a man with a sense of religion, but of a man who lacks such a sense and who is tormented by that lack. When Berryman was converted shortly before his death, it was because of his discovery of what he called a "God of rescue": "He saves men from their situations, off and on during life's pilgrimage, and in the end. I completely bought it, and that's been my position since."[12] That he had been conceiving of God in these terms for a long time, *Homage to Mistress Bradstreet* makes clear. In that poem he pictured God as a literal deus ex machina, but one who had not arrived and will not:[13]

> —I cannot feel myself God waits. He flies
> nearer a kindly world; or he is flown.
> One Saturday's rescue
> won't show.

The note to this stanza directs the reader to movie serials, and defines rescue as "forcible recovery (by the owner) of goods distrained." (A

definition that seems to make a pun of the title of Berryman's unfin-
ished novel, by the way). But in *The Dream Songs* there is no "forcible
recovery by the owner"; Henry must attempt to do all of the rescuing.
Christ is notable in His absence:

> He yelled at me in Greek,
> my God!—It's not his language
> and I'm no good at—his is Aramaic,
> was—I am a monoglot of English
> (American version) and, say pieces from
> a baker's dozen others: where's the bread?
>
> but rising in the Second Gospel, pal:
> The seed goes down, god dies,
> a rising happens,
> some crust, and then occurs   an eating. [48]

The humor here, as so often in *The Dream Songs,* covers a serious and
painful circumstance. Henry, "full of the death of love," is perfectly
familiar with this notion of Christ, but can neither understand it nor
find it in his world. It is "a Greek idea, / troublesome to imaginary
Jews, / like bitter Henry." He is aware of the dying, but not the rising
and the eating: "Where's the bread?" We are told in the following song,
49, that Henry "*wants* to have eaten," but all Henry can do with this
redemptive idea is pun on it.

Thus, although Henry places "crazy bets" with Pascal (referring, of
course, to Pascal's famous "wager"), he is unable to find Pascal's Christ.
He sees a great deal of evidence of Pascal's proof of corruption (Berry-
man's theological leanings are essentially Augustinian and Jansenist),
but very little of his proof of redemption. For example, Henry can pic-
ture in great detail the violence of the Hall-Mills murder case, but

> When to the smokeless mild celestial air
> they came reproved & forgiven, her soul hurrying after his,
> when bright with wisdom of the risen Lord
> enthroned, they swam toward where what may be IS
> and with the rest Mrs Mills, larynx & tongue restored,
> choiring Te Deum, Henry was not there.   [237]

The use of "IS" here is a reference to Lowell's "IS, the whited monster"
of "The Quaker Graveyard in Nantucket," and points to Henry's real
conception of a God who would condone this kind of violence: "What
a monster he must be."

This conflict between the notion of a benevolent God of rescue and the available facts, the aspect of the poem that constitutes the equivocal theodicy that Ricks pointed out, is, like the conflict in Henry's rescue dreams, only partially resolved. Henry never comes to satisfactory terms with God, never achieves the peace of faith or the comfort of redemption. Both father and Father remain unforgiven at the end of the poem. The closest Henry comes to an accommodation with God is in song 383, two songs before the end of the poem: "All men have made mistakes: that includes You." But if Henry cannot achieve a union with or a reconciliation with God, he will be satisfied with its possibility; that is, life not in the frozen season of winter, but the spiritual season of Fall, a season equally corrupt, perhaps, as his desolate winter, but one in which the possibility of salvation, or at least of amelioration, is present. Thus, at the end of section 3, when Henry is "making ready to move on":

> —Henry is tired of the winter,
> & haircuts, & a squeamish comfy   ruin-prone proud
>   national
>   mind,   & Spring (in the city so called).
> Henry likes Fall.
> He would be prepared to live in a world of Fall
> for ever, impenitent Henry.
> But the snows and summers grieve & dream. . . . [77]

And those "snows and summers" dominate much of the rest of the poem, as Henry waits for Fall. At the end of section 6 Henry, again making ready to move on, this time to Ireland and the poem's conclusion, is "Waiting for fall / and the cold fogs thereof / in delicious Ireland" (275). This goal of living in a world of Fall Henry achieves. By accommodating himself to a corrupt world, Henry changes his frozen winter to fall:

> Fall is grievy, brisk. Tears behind the eyes
> almost fall. Fall comes to us as a prize
> to rouse us toward our fate.   [385]

Thus we come to Henry's version of *felix culpa,* the fortunate fall. Although full of grief, Henry's season is not the cold emptiness of winter, but one which points forward, "as a prize / to rouse us toward our fate." (A sad reversal of this pattern is found in a dream song published posthumously, in which Henry longs for the death of winter: "After the pains & glories of the Fall / dead winter. . . .")[14]

Henry, of course, is a part of his world and shares its corruption. He is halved—his every virtue has its corresponding vice. He wants to fight on the side of right, but the enemy exists inside him, and so his wars are civil, as "all wars are civil." He dreams of high virtue and generous deeds, but falls short of achieving them. The worst of his vices, for example, lust, battles the best of his virtues, love, and, until the end of the poem, usually wins. His body has a mind of its own, and, as his friend reminds him, "It's good to be faithful, but it ain't natural / as you knows." His sexual energy is instinctual and allied with his violent impulses, as "This burning to sheathe it" (222) makes clear. But it is also a result of his early fall into self-consciousness, an attempt to recover the "woolen lover" of song 1 and fill the beds growing empty at the end of that song. So, like St. Augustine, Henry strives toward love, but at the same time, like Augustine, asks for one last shot at lust:

> —Vouchsafe me, Sleepless One,
> a personal experience of the body of Mrs Boogry
> before I pass from lust! [69]

This conflict too seems to be resolved near the end of the sequence, as Henry discovers that "We have beaten down the foulest of them, lust . . ." (315). Like Mistress Bradstreet, whom the "prattle of children powers . . . home," Henry achieves a familial love that gains ascendancy over his lust.

Henry's responses to other aspects of his world are also ambivalent. He wants to face his problems squarely, to accept responsibility, to be on the side of life rather than on the side of death. But he is an adept evader, a comic Achilles who sulks more out of fear than out of pride:

> Baseball, & the utter   bloody fucking news,
> converged on miserable Henry, eh?
> Brother, they did.
> Then how did Henry make itself of use?
> apart, I mean, from these nuclear devices H & A.
> Henry hid. [197]

Henry's drinking is part of this pattern of grand evasion, a way of avoiding his problems by distorting the world he perceives: "A maze of drink said: I   will help you through the world. / It is not worse than Hobbes said, nor as bad" (339).

If the world cannot be changed, Henry asks for a change to come to him:

> —Hand me back my crawl,
>
> condign Heaven. Tighten into a ball
> elongate & valved Henry. Tuck him peace.
> Render him sightless,
> or ruin at high rate his crampon focus,
> wipe out his need. Reduce him to the rest of us.   [25]

This is a prayer for regression, a desire to return to infancy ("Hand me back my crawl") or, even better, to a prenatal state ("Tighten into a ball"). But this is just another form of hiding, like his drinking a desire for oblivion, allied to his unsatisfactory suicidal impulses.

Similar to this, but on a more extended scale, is Henry's most spectacular attempt at a radical resolution to his problems in section 4, the "Op. Posth." section. There are overtones here of the epic visit to the Underworld in preparation for future action—"In slack times visit I the violent dead / and pick their awful brains" (88)—but most of the section is devoted to Henry's attempt to avoid responsibility for his guilt by denying and thus overthrowing "His Majesty the Body," for, bodiless, he can commit no crimes:

> I can say no more except that for the record
> I add that all the crimes since all the times he
> died will be due to the breath
>
> of unknown others, sweating in their guilt
> while my client Henry's brow of stainless steel
> rests free, as well it may,
> of all such turbulence. . . .   [86]

So Henry's first attempt at "moving on" after *77 Dream Songs* is, ironically, not a step forward, but a step backward: death as the ultimate regression. For Henry to be free of "all such turbulence" is for him to be stainless, without guilt, but also to be stainless steel, without humanity. This conflict can have no resolution; Henry can only accommodate himself to it as the way things are, and the poem ends with the resigned assertion that there is no "middle ground between things and the soul."

The division of Henry into warring factions is emphasized by the minstrel show banter occasionally found in the poem. (It appears in only about ten percent of the songs but, like the syntactic variations of *Homage to Mistress Bradstreet,* is so impressive that it seems to dominate the work). Henry's striving, idealistic self is undercut by his cynical, wise-guy counterpart who reminds him, when necessary, of the facts. This "friend," this other half of Henry, addresses him as "Bones"—the

end-man Bones of the minstrel show, and the end-man Bones of mortal-
ity: "We hafta *die*. / That is our 'pointed task. Love & die" (36). (Berryman
planned on using the quotation "We were all end-men" as an epigraph
to the poem.) The use of the minstrel show, which Constance Rourke
described as a triumph of comedy with a tragic undertone, is brilliant.
Henry in blackface stands, an "imaginary Negro," as Berryman had stood
in his early short story "The Imaginary Jew," bearing "in the fading
night our general guilt." But as Berryman's fondness for the quotation
"We were all end-men" should indicate, his interest is at least as much
metaphysical as it is social, and probably more so. Henry in blackface is
an American figure, but he is also a descendant of Rimbaud's "nigger,"
a metaphysical slave, one of "the race that sang under torture." For
Henry, as for Rimbaud, "life is the farce we all have to lead,"[15] and the
farce is painful as well as comically absurd.

So Henry, *poète maudit* turned minstrel, jumps Jim Crow, and iden-
tifies with both the physical and spiritual conditions of Rimbaud and
the original Jim Crow,[16]

a strange mixture of pathos and humor. His right shoulder was deformed
and drawn up high; his left leg was gnarled with rheumatism, stiff and
crooked at the knee, so that the Negro walked with a limp, obviously
painful and yet laughable. As he worked, he sang a rather mournful tune
and, at the end of each stanza, gave a queer little jump, setting his "heel-
a-rickin'" as he alighted.

So Carl Wittke on Jim Crow in *Tambo and Bones,* the epigraph to which
became an epigraph to *77 Dream Songs*—"'Go in brack man, de day's
yo' own'"—but which, in the shift from front of book to front of book,
became ironic. Wittke enjoyed this painful grotesque and all the white
men who imitated him in fun; Henry identifies with him, and sees the
desperate irony in the comedy, for to jump Jim Crow is to sing under tor-
ture, and while it may be comic, it isn't any fun:

> That isna Henry limping. That's a hobble
> clapped on mere Henry by the most high GOD
> for the freedom of Henry's soul. [113]

"You perceive I employ a capital initial in the pronoun referring to the
Deity," Melville wrote to Hawthorne, "don't you think there is a slight
dash of flunkeyism in that usage?" A capital initial so used becomes
rebellious. And there is thrice the flunkeyism and thrice the rebellion
in the exaggerated deference paid to "the most high GOD," who, to free
Henry, hobbles him. This rebellious flunkeyism, the strategy of the slaves

of men, is also the strategy of the metaphysical slave. It is at the same time a method of survival and a subversive act:

> Ol' Marster, being bound you do your best
> versus we coons, spare now a cagey John
> a whilom bits that whip. . . .   [51]

And so a whimper becomes a cry of defiance.

But neither Rimbaud's "nigger" nor the blackface minstrels ever spoke quite the way Henry speaks; indeed, before Berryman put the words in his mouth, no one ever spoke like Henry. The language of the poem is, like Henry, a mixture of high seriousness and low comedy, and the juxtaposition of these two elements—often within individual songs—is one of the most striking aspects of the poem. But it is difficult to talk of "the style" of *The Dream Songs,* as if the style were some consistent, coherent aspect of the poem. When we say "style" in speaking of *The Dream Songs* (indeed, in speaking of Berryman's work in general), we mean not the linguistic norm established by the work, but the deviations from that norm, which occur relatively infrequently— the puns, the inversions, and the blackface talk. And what is remarkable about this style is its lack of consistency or coherence, its ability to absorb, in apparently total violation of the principle of decorum, virtually any locution.

But the style is not so much a violation of decorum as it is an extension of it, for the linguistic stew of the style matches perfectly the complexity of Henry's situation and character, at once grave, painful, and funny, stately and outrageous. It is characterized by, among other things, "its patent disregard for grammatical, syntactical, and phonological rule and precedent; its larger capacity . . . for taking in new words and phrases from outside sources and for manufacturing them of its own materials"[17] (Mencken on the American language). Or:[18]

The author was talking negro, using a sort of telegram language, passing all bounds in the suppression of verbs, affecting a ribald humor, condescending to quips and quibbles only worthy of a commercial traveller of the baser sort; then, in a moment, in this tangle of ludicrous conceits, of smirking affectation, would rise a cry of acute pain, like a violoncello string breaking. [Huysmans on Corbière]

I would not of course suggest that either of these quotations is a source for Berryman's language, but they do indicate the two directions in which Berryman's style reaches, and emphasize the important adaptation in *The Dream Songs* of the American tongue to the Symbolists'

concern with the creation of a new language. Like the Rimbaud–Jim
Crow complex, the language of *The Dream Songs* mingles elements
from the modern tradition and the American past. At its best, the styl-
istic deviance of the poem gives the impression that Henry is creating
the language as he goes along, that each painful or comic twist in his
career requires the creation of an expression adequate to it. "Henry in
trouble whirped out lonely whines." "Whirped," the perfect word for
this occasion, exists in no dictionary.

This is the language of the poem at its best, the language that remains
after the poem is read. But the style is not always successful. Indeed (to
quote it yet again), Jarrell's criticism of the language of *The Dispossessed*
is at times an appropriate cricicism of the language of *The Dream Songs:*
"Doing things in a style all its own sometimes seems the primary object
of the poem, and its subject gets a rather spasmodic and fragmentary
treatment."[19] Like other writers of successful idiosyncratic styles, Ber-
ryman occasionally skirts the edges of self-parody. At times the best and
the worst can be found in the same poem:

> When worst got things, how was you? Steady on?
> Wheedling, or shockt her &
> you have been bad to your friend,
> whom not you writing to. You have not listened.
> A pelican of lies
> you loosed: where are you?
>
> Down weeks of evenings of longing
> by hours, NOW, a stoned bell,
> you did somebody: others you hurt short:
> anyone ever did you do good?
> You licking your own old hurt,
> what?   [20]

What Berryman seems to be doing here—and I think this is typical of
the use of stylistic deviance in *The Dream Songs*—is establishing a pat-
tern of regularity and deviance, each highlighting the other. As in *Hom-
age to Mistress Bradstreet,* the stylistic dissonance is resolved in the
grammatically consonant phrases. At the same time, meaning and pattern
are withheld until the resolution. This allows for, among other things,
a multiplicity of meanings, so that not merely words, but whole sentences,
pun. This is essentially the principle of periodicity screwed to its highest
intensity, and the periodic sentence of stanza 2 is a good example. Until
we reach the subject and verb in line 3, "Down weeks" seems to be
the equivalent of "for weeks." The verb, however, adds a layer of mean-
ing—"you did somebody down [for] weeks," etc. "Others you hurt

short" brings out the pun implicit in "longing." Furthermore, the third stanza plays off the language of the second, as God is asked to "hurl down" "something" in order to save the one who has done down somebody.

The regularity and the inversions complement, accent, and illuminate one another; this is the rule for Berryman's style at its best. In the first line of the poem, the inversion serves to emphasize not only the cliché-saving "worst" but also the parallelism between "things" and "you." The slangy and shocking "was," emphasized by both meter and alliteration, halts the reader. Berryman does not allow the perfunctory and mild inquiry, with its overtones of interest in one's health, of "how were you?" (We might go further here, but only with risk, for it is difficult to tell how much weight that "was you" should carry. It is possible, at any rate, that the phrase is more than rough and ungrammatical, that Berryman has Henry here turn from the first or third person to the second in mid-sentence, from considering himself at a comfortable distance —"how was he [I]"—that man I was in the past—to confronting himself directly, as an accuser, "you.") The linguistic confusion in the second line, caused by the tense change and omission of function words, is illuminated by the straightforwardness of the third line—"you have been bad to your friend." The only image in the stanza, "a pelican of lies," is admirably appropriate; one pictures lies flying like fish spat from the large storehouse of the pelican's beak.

The inversion in the fourth line of the second stanza, with its emphasis on "anyone" and "ever," heightens our awareness of Henry's desperation in a way that the flatter "did you ever do anyone good" would not. It also emphasizes, again as normal word order would not, the "did —" formula that Berryman is using in the song: "you did good" in opposition to "you did down." Beneath the word order there is a marvel of effects. But this is not always the case. The fourth line of the first stanza, for example, seems to be inverted for no particular reason. It is neither memorable on its own, nor does it serve any purpose of emphasis. It is as if the inversion were there just to fit the pattern of deviance-regularity, forcing the reader to stumble over "whom not you writing to" simply to get to the smooth ground of "You have not listened."

I have not chosen song 20 absolutely at random, but I do think that it is typical of both the good and the bad elements of the style of *The Dream Songs*. In his introduction to Nashe's *The Unfortunate Traveller*, Berryman wrote that "the notion 'style' points in two contrary directions: toward individuality, the characteristic, and towards inconspicuous expression of its material."[20] Berryman's work obviously falls into the first category; his style is complex and conspicuous. I find unconvincing the argument that the primary purpose of Berryman's style lies at some remove from the notion "meaning," that it is primarily intended to create a world or draw the reader away from a consideration of *The Dream Songs* as "Literature." That it does these things to a certain extent, I would agree, but neither function is sufficient—the style must "mean," it seems to me, in order to be completely justifiable. When it fails to mean, it irritates. But when it succeeds, it does more than merely call attention to itself—it reveals things that, expressed in a different way, would remain hidden.

The title of *The Dream Songs* allows Berryman a great deal of linguistic freedom, of course. The dreamer is an inveterate punner and player with language. But "good poets love bad puns," and we do not really need the title to describe (or defend) the language. The title refers in the first place to dreams as we have learned about them from Freud— the welling up of repressed material in a disguised fashion in sleep. Dreams are caused by a conflict that is of great importance in *The Dream Songs,* the conflict between instinctual needs and the needs of the culture. Indeed, dreams are the battlegrounds of that conflict, for the instinctual material which would conflict with the needs of the culture is allowed in dreams a harmless release. So the title refers to both the purpose and the method of dreams.

That method is similar to the one mentioned in one of the epigraphs, "But there is another method," taken from Olive Schreiner's preface to the second edition of *The Story of an African Farm.* The two methods Miss Schreiner discusses are methods the artist can use to portray "truth." In the first method, the "stage method," characters are wooden, problems are contrived so that easy solutions may be discovered.[21]

But there is another method—the method of life we all lead. Here nothing can be prophesied. There is a strange coming and going of feet. Men appear, act and re-act upon each other, and pass away. When the crisis comes, the man who would fit it does not return. When the curtain falls, no one is ready. When the footlights are brightest, they are blown out: and what the name of the play is no one knows.

One can see why this quotation would have appealed to Berryman, not just for its description of the method, but in details like "When the crisis comes, the man who would fit it does not return"—a perfect description of Christ in *The Dream Songs:* " 'O come on down. O come on down.' / Clear whom *he* meant" (21).

But one should not equate this "method" with "structure." There is a great deal of "coming and going of feet" in the poem, but this is a more appropriate description of the atmosphere of the poem than it is of the structure. Randomness, although it is certainly present in *The Dream Songs,* is more the lack of structure than a structural principle. At the same time, as tantalizing as the thought might be, there seems to be no tightly knit but hidden or "secret" structure to *The Dream Songs.* Critics have presented theses about the structure of the poem based on things as divergent as numerology and the logic of Hegel, but none is fully convincing.[22] Furthermore, Berryman's own comments on the structure of the poem are, like his comments on other aspects of the work, sometimes misleading. For example, in an interview published in the *Harvard Advocate* in 1969, Berryman, responding to the question, "So in fact, the book has no plot?" said:[23]

Those are fighting words. It has a plot. Its plot is the personality of Henry as he moves on in the world. Henry gains ten years. At one time his age is given as forty-one, 'Free, black and forty-one,' and at a later point he's fifty-one. So the poem spans a large area, you see that.

Henry's personality is indeed important in the poem, but the age differences are a relatively minor aspect of that personality. Henry is forty-one in song 40 (and, presumably, the earlier songs), but he turns fifty-one in song 104, so the "large area" spanned by those ten years is actually quite small.

In another interview Berryman said that "each book [of the poem] is rather well unified."[24] This too, it seems to me, is a bit misleading. It depends on what one means by "unified." One can identify general trends in specific books, but very little tightly knit structure. Book 6, for example, is framed by Delmore Schwartz's death—there are twelve elegiac songs at the beginning and a song on the anniversary of his death, "July 11," near the end. It is the most agonized and despairing book of the volume, and can be said to have a specific theme: survival in "the country of the dead." However, aside from the beginning and the end, and a few obvious examples in between, there seems to be no particular reason why one song must follow or precede another, or, for that matter, why many of those songs must be in that book and no other. The book is loosely unified by theme and subject matter, but many individual parts of the book could be juggled around without seriously affecting the structure.

I think that this could safely be said about the other books in the volume and about the volume as a whole. It has a beginning and an end and a general development from beginning to end; it is loosely unified by theme, subject matter, imagery, and, of course, Henry, but many individual songs could be juggled around without affecting that loose unity. As I have noted, Berryman apparently intended to end the sequence much earlier than he actually did. Song 385 was originally published as "161: The Last Song." There is also some internal evidence supporting this theory. At the end of book 5 Henry is attempting to forgive his father for the pain he has caused, and is looking forward to "the last dream, the last song" (137). Perhaps two brief sections chronicling Henry's discovery of continuity and love were to conclude the volume. But Berryman kept going, confusing as he went his life and his poem. As a result, books 6 and 7, which contain well over half of the songs, dominate the volume, and Henry's growth from forty-one to fifty-one, recounted in the earlier books, becomes less important than his mental growth during the years when he is fifty and fifty-one, recounted in books 6 and 7.

Furthermore, much of the book is static. We may talk about "plot," meaning "general development," but the word is best kept within quotation marks; there is certainly little plot in the novelistic sense. What "plot" there is is generally provided at the beginning and end of each section; the middle consists of variations on the themes that we have discussed earlier. Nevertheless, the poem is not totally chaotic, formless, or incoherent. There are, as we have seen, many recurring images and situations, and there is a general pattern to the poem. The first three books are introductory and come closest to resembling in structure Olive Schreiner's "method." "The plot" of 77 Dream Songs, writes William Meredith, "is the discovery of Henry's whole identity, by him and by us."[25] The book sets before us the whole ragged ball of twine that comprises that identity: Henry's loss, the elements of his world, his responses to that loss and that world. But the ball of twine is not quite so ragged as it appears. While certain themes, such as loss, run through all three books, each book emphasizes, by the number of songs and their placement at the beginning and ending, a particular aspect of Henry's character or situation. The first emphasizes Henry's lust. The second, which is the first book explicitly to mention Henry's father's suicide, and which is dominated by the war imagery that is continued throughout the poem, emphasizes violence, both Henry's own repressed violence and the violence of the world at large, "our wounds to time." The third book emphasizes Henry's poetry and the potentially restorative value of poetry. This is reinforced by Berryman's use of tree imagery, introduced in the first poem of the volume: "Once in a sycamore I was glad / all at the top, and I sang." This innocent Tree of Life is transformed by Henry's fall into a Tree of Death, and Henry in a tree becomes Henry up a tree, Henry as treed 'coon, or lynched "coon." The original state of bliss becomes a state of helplessness and violence. Rather than singing, "Men psalm. Man palms his ears and moans" (41). But Henry strives through his art to recreate the original tree, which becomes the "flashing & bursting tree" of song 75, which "strike[s] the passers from despair." (Later, in song 328, Henry, nearing triumph, "flourisht like a sycamore tree," having recreated the Tree of Life not just in his art, but in his life as well.) So there are unifying elements in these first three books, and even a "plot" that goes a bit beyond the discovery of Henry's identity, but one that is very little more complicated than the "plot" of those five dream songs published in *TLS* in 1959. What is more important here than structure—and this is generally true in the later books as well—is the depiction of a world, and Henry's almost ad hoc attempts to come to terms with it. *77 Dream Songs* could be more greatly unified, I think, without changing the depiction of that world; and this is also true of the book as a whole.

The next three books are, in terms of development, almost as static as the first three. At the end of book 3 Henry is "making ready to move on," but book 4, as I have noted earlier, presents a regression rather than a progression. In book 5, which begins with "Room 231: the forth week" (punning, I suspect, not only on "forth" but also on "week"— Henry gets "the rare Order of Weak" in song 93), Henry does begin to move on, and begins to make some progress as he faces, rather than hides from, his environment. But even this progress is emotional or spiritual rather than narrative—Henry simply begins to feel better about some things. In book 3 he had discovered the restorative value of art, and now he begins to discover the importance of his family. Henry is moving toward the realization that Berryman's earlier poet-heroes had come to: that love and work are the only means of coping with his environment. So poems about Henry's family (there were only three in the first seventy-seven) begin to appear more frequently. The birth of Henry's son, for example, brings a temporary end to Henry's winter landscape:

> Behold I bring you tidings of great joy—
> especially now that the snow & gale are still—
> for Henry is delivered.
> Not only is he delivered from the gale
> but he has a little one. He's out of jail
> also. It is a boy.   [124]

The birth of the child is redemptive, as the allusion to Christ's birth in the first line makes clear—Henry is spiritually delivered as the child is physically delivered. We have seen this sort of thing before, in *Homage to Mistress Bradstreet,* and we will see it again in section 7 of this poem.

But this particular use of the "saving child" is confusing, for one of the references to Henry's family in *77 Dream Songs* is to "my second wife & my son" (54). Is the son of song 124 the same son referred to in the earlier song, or a new one? If it is a new one, why is there no indication that there is another? If it is the same son (Berryman had only one son, and so one is drawn to this alternative), then great unresolved questions of structure arise, for we are thrown back into the nonnarrative parts of the first 77, given an event that occurred before the events of many of the earlier songs. I suspect that in fact Berryman was simply not interested in these questions. The birth is less an exterior event than it is an interior event. What matters is not the narrative direction the birth of a child might provide; what matters is its impact on Henry's mental life, the fact that the delivery of the child delivers Henry. This kind of narrative confusion is a relatively minor flaw, perhaps (one must finally ignore it in order to get on with the poem), but it is annoying, and is the kind of flaw that makes *The Dream Songs* less successful than *Homage to Mistress Bradstreet*.

I have already discussed my suspicion that Berryman intended to end the poem with brief sixth and seventh books. The emphasis on Henry's family in book 5 (a sure sign that Henry's state is improving) is perhaps another indication of this. At any rate, Berryman did not end the poem—he went on in fact to write more songs than he had already written. Perhaps it was Delmore Schwartz's death that changed the development of the poem; most likely that and other factors that we don't know about were at work. Speaking of the end of book 3, Berryman said that Henry "was 'making ready to move on.' Well, I was already well ahead of him."[26] But with book 6 that relationship begins to change, and the tenuous distinction between Berryman and Henry at times breaks down completely, as in "Henry's Mail." The style, in at least some of the songs, becomes simpler and flatter; there are still a great many aspects of the style as established in earlier books, but there are fewer than before. It is as if a second poem had been begun and was running alongside the first; a poem implicit, indeed, throughout the songs, but not explicit: a poem about Berryman writing a poem about Henry. Interviewed shortly after *The Dream Songs* was finished, Berryman said, "Mostly, I'm through with Henry, but the minute I say that, pains course through me. I can't bear to be rid of that admirable outlet, that marvelous way of making your mind known to many other people."[27] And that, indeed, is what the poem had frequently become: "admirable outlet."

But this does not mean that the fictive aspects of Henry's character disappear entirely. Indeed, the "plot" of Henry's life comes to a fitting conclusion in book 7. Henry resolves some of the conflicts that had tormented him in earlier books and comes to the realization that some of those conflicts cannot be resolved. I have used the word "triumph" to describe this conclusion, and so I think it is, but perhaps the words from one of Berryman's first poems, "Letter to His Brother," are more appropriate: "responsible delight." That poem, which had described a world about which the poet could make no "hopeful prophecy," had ended:

> May love, or its image in work,
> Bring you that dignity to know the dark
> And so to gain responsible delight.

Berryman never strayed from that early, Freudian idea, and Henry comes to a similar conclusion, more colloquially expressed:

> Working & children & pals are the point of the thing,
> for the grand sea awaits us, which will then us toss
> & endlessly us undo.   [303]

That "grand sea," introduced in the very first song ("Hard on the land wears the strong sea") and associated with Henry's father's death (and death in general) in many subsequent songs, represents the ultimate threat of the poem and one which cannot be avoided. It will "us toss / & endlessly us undo." Over against that threat, however, now lies the consolation and continuity represented by Henry's daughter, whose presence dominates this last section. The book is similar to the last section of *Homage to Mistress Bradstreet*—like Mistress Bradstreet, Henry discovers the value of the family as a source of love and solace, and accommodates himself to the things he cannot change, especially the fact of mortality.

Throughout *The Dream Songs* death has been seen as the ultimate loss and the ultimate injustice. Henry's own death by suicide was seen as the ultimate escape from responsibility. Henry now looks forward to death, not as an escape (suicide is again rejected in this book) but with a resigned acceptance. "The wind blows hard from our past into our future," Henry says in a lovely line, "and we are that wind, except that the wind's nature / was not to last" (282). His attitude toward his coming death is much less sanguine than Mistress Bradstreet's—"Wandering pacemaker, unsteadying friend, / in a redskin calm I wait: / beat when you will our end"—for Henry is uncertain about an afterlife. Nevertheless, when Henry does dream his final death (as Berryman said, "at the end of the poem he is still alive, and in fairly good condition, after having died himself *again*"),[28] it is described as a "terrible gay / occasion" (382), a moment of Yeatsian tragic gaiety, as a Yeatsian dancer (perhaps the "high heroine" of the earlier songs) "dances Henry away" from his pain. Earlier Henry had looked forward to his "blessed discharge" (281)—a remarkably appropriate word combining the images of his world as hospital and battleground—and now he sees how that will be achieved, with "'Give!' & 'Ow!'" but finally with "All is well."

The last two poems of the volume demand, by their contrasts, to be read together. The first (384) points backward through *The Dream Songs* to the very beginning of Henry's problems, his father's suicide. Henry has hefted the ax that he uses here in earlier songs, and he has described his dream world as a place "where foes are attacked with axes" (352). Indeed, Henry's barely repressed violence was expressed in terms of hacking as early as song 29. (Compare stanza 34 of *Homage to Mistress Bradstreet* for similar imagery.) Here the ax is used in imagination ("I'd like to . . .") to release his pent-up violence and kill, not his father, but his obsession with his father, the center of the pattern of loss that Henry has lived with, to "fell it on the start."

Henry cuts himself off from his father and his past and then sees himself as father and looks to the future. From the fall of the ax he looks to the fall of the leaves. The tone of the last poem is as calm as the tone of 384 is hysterical. It is a poem of acceptance, of thanksgiving, both figuratively and literally; and if thanksgiving means that "Everywhere in enormous numbers turkeys will be dying," Henry will not rail at the fact. For Henry, like Mistress Bradstreet, who realized that "hangnails, piles, fibs, life's also," has come to accept the often painful contrasts between the actual and the ideal, the physical and the spiritual, between "things and the soul." Ralph Hodgson is invoked here less as a poet, I suspect, than as a kind man, a benevolent presence in Henry's house, "good Ralph Hodgson," who in Eliot's "Five-Finger Exercises" is a patron of those who fly and sing—he "has 999 canaries, / And round his head finches and fairies / In jubilant rapture skim." "I don't try to reconcile anything," Berryman quoted Hodgson in an essay published in 1965, "this is a damned strange world";[29] and neither, any longer, does Henry try to reconcile anything. "I suppose the word would be, we must submit. / *Later*," Henry had written many songs before, and he does submit in this song, perhaps not with "jubilant rapture," but at least calmly, accepting the irreconcilable, accepting even the fact that a father (and perhaps a Father) will have to scold the child he loves.

The Dream Songs is not a completely successful poem. *Homage to*

Mistress Bradstreet, more compact, more coherent, is a more successful work. There is not enough narrative in *The Dream Songs* to hold such a long work together, and what narrative there is is often confused. The methods of organization which are essentially lyric—recurrent images and language—are not developed consistently enough; there is just enough development to force us to read the poem as a whole, but not enough for us to see it as a totally coherent whole. The poem was too available to the daily events of Berryman's life, perhaps. The attempt to turn his life into myth succeeds best when Berryman abstracts himself from Henry, by putting him in a fictive environment—up a tree, or dead, or even simply bored—or by treating him ironically or humorously—showing us Henry hungering after a woman in a restaurant, or suffering the effects of a "truly first-class drill" in a dentist's chair. Unfortunately, this attempt does not always succeed. But despite its faults, the poem remains a considerable achievement; Henry, his dream world, and his language remain in the mind after reading, indelible.

5

LATE POEMS

Berryman did not stop writing dream songs after the publication of *His Toy, His Dream, His Rest*—"that admirable outlet" continued to attract him, apparently—but no new songs were added to the collected *Dream Songs* (1969), and most of his energies were being directed elsewhere. He was, at various times between 1968 and his death in 1972, working on a translation of Sophocles, a book on Shakespeare (on which he had been working, on and off, for decades), a life of Christ for children, and a novel, "'the first part of which was about a man trying to solve his inner problems, the second part about the sickness of the world today,'"[1] which was published unfinished as *Recovery* after his death. He was also, he declared in a press interview occasioned by his sharing the Bollingen award with Karl Shapiro, working on two books of poetry.[2] Short poems, but conceived from very early on as separate books. Not satisfied with the notion of simply writing lyrics, Berryman organized his short poems as he was writing them into a larger structure.

The first collection, *Love & Fame,* appeared in 1970, and shocked most critics. The jacket blurb announced "a style new for Berryman, new for anybody," and so indeed it seemed to be. Speaking in propria persona, Berryman bragged and strutted, alternately telling the reader how famous he was and what an active sex life he had. Falling on the ready-made pun, reviewers spoke, generally with distaste, of Berryman's name dropping and pants dropping. The book elicited not simply negative appraisals, but frequently hostile and mocking comments. The most hostile critics spoke of being "disgusted" by the subject matter; friendly critics worried that Berryman had lost his talent.

Berryman was himself unsure of the quality of this new collection.

"They were so weird," he said, "so unlike all my previous work that I was a little worried"[3] before they were published. In the English edition and the second American edition, he "killed some of the worst poems,"[4] three "sexual" poems and three "political" poems.

At the same time, though, although he did not of course defend the quality of the poems, Berryman felt it necessary—once again—to correct some misconceptions, the most serious being the refusal to admit any irony into this bragging version of the search for love and fame. The book, he explained, was "a whole, each of the four movements criticizing backward the preceding, until Part 4 wipes out altogether all earlier presentations of the 'love' and 'fame' of the ironic title."[5] The book takes the form of the virtually mythic conversion narrative, the amoral youth discovering God and the error of his ways. Some reviewers noticed this (Jerome Mazzaro, principally, who compared the book to Augustine's *Confessions*[6]), but most did not. This was not entirely the fault of the reviewers, for Berryman relies on the progress of the book rather than on immediate irony to distance his "mature" self from his youth. The sequence is written by a man who has come to see the futility of the notions of "love" and "fame" that he had as a young man, but we seldom get a glimpse of that wiser man in the early sections. With a few exceptions, the early poems are straightforward and written from the point of view of the youth.

There is no noticeable irony, for example, in the description of Berryman's receiving a C in Professor Neff's course and almost not graduating from Columbia. His statement that receiving a C placed him "squarely in the middle of Hell" seems to be straightforward. "Is this," wrote Robert Phillips, "really sufficient impetus to place a soul 'squarely in the middle of Hell'?"[7] Of course it is not. But the problem, it seems to me, is cleared up in "The Hell Poem" in section 3. The contrast between this very real hell of "anguishes; / gnawings" and the egocentric youth's notion of hell in section 1 is extreme, and does indeed, as Berryman said, "wipe out" that early conception.

Berryman never claimed the status of a long poem for *Love & Fame*, but it must be read, as he said, as a whole. Indeed, the book is structurally more satisfying than Berryman's major long poem, *The Dream Songs*, for there are few obtrusions into the narrative, and the story told is fairly clear. That story is not very different from the stories told in Berryman's other works. The book describes the development of a poetic sensibility struggling against both outer and inner obstacles. In his earlier work, though, much greater attention is paid to the outer obstacles—the mad culture the poet finds himself a part of—than is paid here. In *Love & Fame* there are some poems about American society, but what is most important about that society is Berryman's isolation from it. In school and at college he is, despite his efforts to the contrary ("I made at Columbia a point of being popular"[8]) an exile. His father's suicide separates him from the normal home life of his friends, and he is more comfortable in Harlem listening to blues singers than he is on Morningside Heights.

However, most of the obstacles in these early sections are inner. Berryman's own misconceptions and his own frightening lust are the real enemies. His ambition and his lust are related—they are both attempts to impose his massive ego on the world around him. His poetic drive and his sexual drive are brought together in "Two Organs." The first organ is feminine, Plato's uterus, which the young Berryman thinks he resembles:

> Plato's uterus, I say,
> an animal passionately longing for children
>
> and, if long unsatisfied after puberty,
> prone to range angrily, blocking the air passages
> & causing distress & disease.
> For 'children' read: big fat fresh original &
> characteristic poems.   [p. 16]

The second organ is masculine:

> An eccentric friend, a Renaissance scholar, sixty-odd,
> unworldly, he writes limericks in Medieval Latin,
> stood up in the rowboat fishing to take a leak
> & exclaimed as he was about it with excitement
>
> "I wish my penis was big enough for this whole lake!"
> My phantasy precisely at twenty:
> to satisfy at once all Barnard & Smith
> & have enough left over for Miss Gibbs's girls.   [p. 17]

(Young Berryman, besides being a rake, is also a snob: he wishes to satisfy the Barnard and Smith girls before turning to their working class sisters at Katherine Gibbs's Secretarial School). Both of these notions, both parts of Berryman's hermaphroditic drive, are wiped out in following sections, although it is his lust which brings him to the spiritual and emotional crisis that is at the center of the volume.

The beginning of this crisis is described in "Damned." The word is used seriously; this is not the undergraduate's hell of a C, but a true sense of emotional and spiritual damnation—"The Hell Poem" follows shortly. "Damned" describes the conception of Berryman's illegitimate child. In "Her & It," the first poem in the volume, Berryman had said, rather cavalierly, "I'll bet she now has seven lousy children. / (I've three myself, one being off the record.)" This attitude—"seven lousy children" —changes during the course of the volume. In "Message" children are seen as being of central importance: "Children! Children! form the point of all. / Children & high art" (p. 57). Here, real children and poetic children, the offspring of "Plato's uterus," are equally important. The line should sound familiar, for the sentiment was for a long time a part of Berryman's work. But in "Damned" the child is not a form of solace, but a reminder of his adultery. The point of view in the poem shifts: there are several "Berrymans" in *Love & Fame,* and there are at least two here. In the first stanza Berryman's "mistress" (the poem seems to indicate that their relationship was limited to a single night; it was no doubt one of many such relationships) is pregnant. In the next three stanzas Berryman recalls the night of conception:

> She came again & again, twice ejecting me
> over her heaving. I turned my head aside
> to avoid her goddamned tears,
> getting in my beard. [p. 68]

This Berryman is simply a bastard. Turning his head "to avoid her goddamned tears," he is the logical result of the youthful Berryman who had thought only of self-gratification. It is this, I think, which makes Berryman a "damned" character. The Berryman of the following stanza is the Berryman of the present, the Berryman of the last line of the poem, and he is a very different man from the adulterer Berryman:

> I am busy tired mad lonely & old.
> O this has been a long long night of wrest.

The "long long night of wrest" in this marvelous couplet is metaphorical. It is Berryman's dark night of the soul, and one which has a way yet to go, through the darkness of "Despair" and the hell sequence.

"Despair" is one of the finest poems in the volume. It begins with flat statement, perfectly appropriate to its subject:

> It seems to be DARK all the time.
> I have difficulty walking.
> I can remember what to say to my seminar
> but I don't know that I want to. [p. 72]

The accretion of these bleak statements in the following two stanzas, one clipped sentence to a line, presents one of the most convincing depictions of despair in literature, one that is deepened by the contrast in the fourth stanza of a brief hope:

> Crackles! in darkness HOPE; & disappears.

The metrical regularity of the line—the only line of iambic pentameter (with a trochaic substitution in the first foot) in the poem—and the syntactic deviance print the brief lightning of hope on the mind. Even the typography emphasizes the contrast, the small capitals of HOPE balancing the small capitals of DARK in the first stanza. What provides this hope is his daughter: "I am in love with my excellent baby." The notion of love has changed radically from the beginning.

This notion is carried over into the institutional sequence which follows "Despair." The light of hope is provided by caring for someone outside of yourself, not by avoiding their "goddamned tears." Thus, it is important that one of the first things we learn in "The Hell Poem" is "I like nearly all the rest of them too" (p. 73). Marjorie Perloff, in *The Poetic Art of Robert Lowell,* has compared Berryman's "hospital poems" with Lowell's, specifically contrasting "Waking in the Blue" with "The Hell Poem." After noting the similarities of the "surface features" in the two poems, Professor Perloff points out that an important difference between the two is that Lowell is a participant in what he describes and that he "moves toward some measure of self-insight and understanding," while Berryman, in a poem which suffers from an "arbitrariness of detail," is simply "a camera, recording what he perceives . . . as so much raw data."[9] Berryman is much like a camera in this poem, although I do not think, as we shall see, that this is a fault. The statement about "arbitrariness of detail," however, is not entirely accurate. While some of the details of the poem are arbitrary—simply setting the scene—others are, when the poem is read in context, significant. The statement that "They can't have matches," for example, takes on significance when one recalls the penultimate line of the preceding poem, "Despair": "There are no matches" [in Berryman's spiritual darkness]. The matches are more a spiritual than a physical tinder.

One might also dispute Professor Perloff's statement that "the fact that 'It's all girls this time' doesn't really make much difference to the poet or, for that matter, to the reader,"[10] for in those girls Berryman is seeing the concrete results of the heartless behavior he had earlier so enthusiastically engaged in:

> It's all girls this time. The elderly, the men,
> of my former stays have given way to girls,
> fourteen to forty, raucous, racing the halls,
> cursing their paramours & angry husbands.   [p. 74]

It is as if the younger Berryman's mistresses had come back to haunt
him, "cursing their paramours" as he had once cursed them and their
"goddamned tears"; the women blend with the "witches" of the follow-
ing stanza. But there is a great difference in Berryman's attitude here,
for he cares about these girls: "Will day glow again to these tossers, and
to me?" This is the reason for Berryman's being like a camera in this
poem: his attention is finally, after two and a half sections of self-
preoccupation, directed as much outward as inward. In a sense, by mere-
ly asking the question he answers it, for care brings its own light with it.
This is explicitly stated in the following poem, "Death Ballad," which
has the epigraph "I don't care," when Berryman tells the suicidal Tyson
and Jo to

> take up, outside your blocked selves, some small thing
> that is moving
> & wants to keep on moving
> & needs therefore, Tyson, Jo, your loving.   [p. 76]

Caring is life, not caring is death, and Berryman's rebirth is a direct re-
sult of this discovery.

The course of "love" in this volume ends in the *Eleven Addresses to
the Lord,* for Berryman discovers love not only in his family, as in his
earlier works, but also in God. "I fell back in love with you, Father"
(p. 95) echoes and wipes out the very first line of the volume: "I fell
in love with a girl." But what of "fame"? It too, I think, is transformed
—and radically so—by the end of the volume. The early Berryman's no-
tion of "fame" is, like his notion of love, a form of ego-gratification,
the imposition of his ego on the world around him. The "children" of
"Plato's uterus" are described as "big fat fresh original & characteristic
poems." "Original & characteristic": poems that would assert the poet's
presence. The form that this assertion would take is more specifically
described by a sentence quoted from R. P. Blackmur in "Olympus":

> "The art of poetry
> is amply distinguished from the manufacture of verse
> by the animating presence in the poetry
> of a fresh idiom: language

so twisted & posed in a form
that it not only expresses the matter in hand
but adds to the stock of available reality." [18]

This is in fact an excellent description of Berryman's verse. But it is a description that is both implicitly and explicitly rejected at the end of *Love & Fame.* The notion of poetry and self-assertion is replaced by the notion of prayer and self-abnegation. Berryman's description of his "morning prayer" in the first of the *Eleven Addresses* is important: "It does not aim at eloquence." What is important in prayer is that it express "with precision everything that most matters." Berryman has moved, by section 4, from creation to the contemplation of creation. God is addressed as "Master of beauty, craftsman of the snowflake," and before such an artist Berryman humbles himself.

Berryman's religious poetry has been criticized, not so much as poetry, but for its lack of sincerity. "I am not convinced of the poet's repentance," wrote Robert Phillips, going on to say that "Berryman's Christian mystic, like the figure of Henry House, was yet another false one behind which to hide."[11] This seems unnecessary. The quality of Berryman's religious poems is uneven, but at his best Berryman was as good a religious poet as he was any other kind of poet. Some of the *Eleven Addresses to the Lord* are extraordinary. The third is perhaps the best. It begins:

> Sole watchman of the flying stars, guard me
> against my flicker of impulse lust: teach me
> to see them as sisters & daughters. Sustain
> my grand endeavors: husbandship & crafting.

and ends:

> Cross am I sometimes with my little daughter:
> fill her eyes with tears. Forgive me, Lord.
> Unite my various soul,
> sole watchman of the wide & single stars. [88]

The contrast between the "flying stars" and "my flicker of impulse lust" caught up at the end as Berryman asks to be united as the "single stars" are, the play on "soul," implicit in the first line, explicit in the last two, and the simplicity of the language unite to make this an admirable poem. Without trying to be eloquent, it is: it says what must be said precisely.

Love & Fame is far from being the aesthetic botch that most reviewers found it to be . But this is not to say that it is Berryman's finest work. There is a problem with this "wiping out" strategy, for after the sensibility of the early poems is wiped out, there is very little left. There is very little stylistic attraction in the first two sections. Had the young Berryman been presented as a slightly more despicable character, the volume would have been improved. One will return to the unpleasant Berryman of "Damned" as one returns to some of Browning's monologues, for the monstrousness and the unattractive vitality of the poem; but most of the early poems present a sensibility without vitality. Young Berryman is not evil enough to attract, and, once or twice read, the anecdotes lose much of their power. The poems are necessary—the second half of the book depends upon them—but they are too often simply straw men, put up in order to be knocked down. The structure of the volume is satisfying, but the early components of that structure, by and large, are not.

In *Delusions, Etc.*, published posthumously but seen through proof by Berryman, there is a thematic unity of a sort, but no clear overarching structure. When poems fail, and quite a few do, they do so on their own, without any narrative compensation. It is true that section 4, the only section with a title, is called "Scherzo," but I would hesitate to claim a symphonic or sonata structure for the book. Individual sections are fairly well unified, but beyond that the book is more of a collection than were Berryman's earlier volumes. The full title of the book is *Delusions, Etc. of John Berryman*, but the delusions are not Berryman's alone. The chief delusion is man's thinking—the pride he takes in his rational faculties. Berryman's work had always been romanticist, and here that romanticism is quite blatant, but curiously mixed: at times Berryman sounds like Emerson, at other times like Melville.

"I don't try to reconcile anything," Berryman had approvingly quoted Ralph Hodgson, "this is a damned strange world";[12] and that is how Henry had ended, looking to Ralph Hodgson and not trying to reconcile "things and the soul." But the conflict that he had ended for Henry did not end for himself. Berryman *did* try to reconcile things: reason and faith, science and religion, the existence of evil and the notion of a benevolent God, and *Delusions, Etc.* is largely a record of that attempt. Hence, the Emersonian-Melvillian contrast: in some poems Berryman does seem to have reconciled these things, in others he recognizes, with pain, that he cannot.

"The passion for secrets," as Berryman describes it in "Gislebertus' Eve," the Faustian desire *to know,* is at the center of the problem. In "Year's End, 1970," Berryman had written:[13]

Gislebertus: Eve deluded brought down on us Evil.
How now shall we encounter His presence again?

He returns to Gislebertus's version of the Fall in "Gislebertus' Eve":[14]

> She snaked out a soft
> small willing hand, curved her ivory fingers on
> a new taste sensation, in reverie over
> something other,
> sank her teeth in, and offered him a bite.
>
> I too find it delicious.

The diction here is nicely worked: Eve contains the serpent in her action, and the apple contains in its description the adman's "new taste sensation," the debasement of civilization that it will cause. The result of this fall is described in the third stanza:

> So now we see where we are, which is all-over
> we're nowhere, son, and suffering we know it,'
> rapt in delusion. . . .

"Rapt in delusion" points to a familiar antinomy of Berryman's—the delusion is pleasant, and it is responsible for great human scientific accomplishments (Leonardo, Darwin, Freud, and Niels Bohr are mentioned). But it is nonetheless delusion, a point emphasized by several other poems in the volume.

Man's thinking—the scientific attitude taken by itself—is, Berryman says in "A Usual Prayer," "eighteen-tenths deluded" (62). The notion that we can "know" the world around us by observing and thinking is simply not true. "Certainty before Lunch" explores this misconception:

> Ninety percent of the mass of the Universe
> (90%!) may be gone in collapsars. . . . [65]

"May be"; but we cannot be certain that "collapsars" (black holes) even exist. The "may be" of the first stanza is answered by the "barely possible *may not* / BE" of the last. Thought cannot bring certainty; it can only point out probability (appropriately enough, Berryman is going for a walk with "the probability man"). The scientist is thus, ironically, for all of his rational thought and higher mathematics, forced to intuit the existence of black holes, just as the theologian must intuit the existence of God. Certainty can only be provided by an irrational leap of faith:

> My Lord, I'm glad we don't
> on x or y depend for Your being there.
> I know You are there. The sweat is, I am here.

We cannot argue the existence of God from the evidence of our senses; the gulf between "things and the soul" is impassable. God is "there," but "The sweat is, I am here," in a "flowerless April snow."

Elsewhere in the volume, though, in an implicitly transcendental manner, Berryman attempts to use science as the first step on the road to knowing God. When men intuit quasars, they must understand that this is God working through them. Science is properly used not as an end in itself, but as a springboard for the leap of faith; Berryman uses facts, as Whitman put it, to "enter by them to an area of my dwelling." Thus, scientific terminology becomes a source of metaphor for Berryman, one that is most evident in the first section of the volume, his "layman's winter mockup" of the Holy Office:

> I am like your sun, Dear, in a state of shear—
> parts of my surface are continually slipping past others,
> not You, not You. O I may, even, wave
> in crisis like a skew Wolf-Rayet star.   [p. 5]

Here Berryman is using brief metaphysical conceits. The comparison of himself to the sun is appropriate, and although it is not developed very fully, it is developed enough to make it effective. The comparison to the Wolf-Rayet star, however appropriate it may be, is not effective, for the metaphor is not developed enough. A conceit demands elaboration, and here there is not even the minimal elaboration that there was in the comparison to the sun.

The scientific language in this section sometimes obtrudes, either because it is not sufficiently developed, as with the Wolf-Rayet star, or because there is too much of it, as in the first poem:

> Let us rejoice on our cots, for His nocturnal miracles
> antique outside the Local Group & within it
> & within our hearts in it, and for quotidian miracles
> parsecs-off yielding to the Hale reflector.   [p. 3]

The point of the scientific language is to use it to transcend science; but such a fearful agglomeration of it emphasizes the science at the expense of the devotion and the poetry.

Over against the scientist stands the figure of the artist, who rises above mere thought:

Thinking presides, some think now,—only presides—
at the debate of the Instincts; but presides,
over powers, over love, hurt-back.
You grumbled: "Religion and Figured Bass are closed concepts.
Don't argue." [p. 22]

Beethoven is quoted in the poem ("Beethoven Triumphant") as describing himself as "brain-owner," but his art goes beyond the powers of thought:

You made throats swallow
and shivered the backs of necks.
You made quiver with glee, at will; not long.
This world is of male energy male pain. [p. 22]

As a result of this Beethoven achieves immortality, but it is the immortality of the artist—his "male energy," transformed into art, that lives in us. The elegy for the artist is one of Berryman's most familiar themes. But oddly enough, the four elegies in this volume do not quite fit with what I take to be the thematic significance of art in the book, which is that the goal of art is greater understanding of God. *"On parle toujours de l'art religieux,"* states one of the epigraphs, *"L'art est religieux."* This is the subject of one poem, "Ecce Homo," in which the contemplation of a photograph of a painted crucifix leads Berryman to an understanding of Christ's humanity as well as his divinity. This aspect of art is not really touched on in the elegies. Beethoven's world and his immortality are "male energy male pain." These elegies are more reminiscent of *The Dream Songs* than *"l'art est religieux."* This does not hurt the poems themselves, of course, but it does weaken what little unity the volume has.

The use of scientific language is not the only aspect of linguistic experimentation in the volume; there are others, some quite effective, some unfortunate. The ability to juxtapose the formal and the colloquial, exhibited so successfully in *The Dream Songs,* is evident here as well. To place in the formal and solemn "Minnesota Thanksgiving" the word "Yippee!" is an audacious stroke and, I think, an effective one, as is the use of "hot diggity" in the poem to Emily Dickinson. But such experiments are not always successful. "Unknowable? perhaps not altogether," the subject of which is "Adonai of rescue," ends: "still / we're trans-acting with You" (p. 60). "Trans-acting" serves to vulgarize the poem's subject, not to enliven it or bring it down to earth. "Yippee!"

is the explosion of human, childlike, and perfectly charming enthusiasm; "trans-acting" strikes a false note— it sounds artificially informal and "hip," like "Are you running with me, Jesus?"

There are, indeed, some very weak poems in this collection. The book has been compared favorably with *Love & Fame*, in both reviews and criticism, but I must believe that this is due less to the poetry than to the attitude Berryman seemed to strike in each volume. In *Love & Fame* Berryman appeared to be a bragging oaf and the appearance hid the poetry. In *Delusions, Etc.* Berryman is "properly humble," and this too seems to have hidden the poetry, for the best one can say of the volume is that it is very uneven. The chief failure of the book, moreover, is not one of sensibility, but one of language—it is not that Berryman is too "confessional" or that his conversion is not convincing, but that his artistic experiments too frequently do not succeed.

When the language does work, as we have seen, it can be very effective. Perhaps the most successful poem in the book, though, is one in which the language calls the least attention to itself—"He Resigns," in which the tone is flat, bleak, and despairing:

> Age, and the deaths, and the ghosts.
> Her having gone away
> in spirit from me. Hosts
> of regrets come & find me empty.
>
> I don't feel this will change.
> I don't want any thing
> or person, familiar or strange.
> I don't think I will sing
>
> any more just now;
> or ever. I must start
> to sit with a blind brow
> above an empty heart.   [p. 40]

It is difficult to read this poem in light of Berryman's suicide. However, it is questionable psychology to read the poems as an adumbration of that act. It was written well before his suicide; he had written poems like it in the past; nevertheless, it expresses pure empty despair so well that we think we know that that's just how it felt and feels. But the artistry that helps to express that despair is highly wrought. The iambs of the repeated "I don't" phrases in the second stanza beat the feeling into the reader, as does the pyrrhic-spondaic combination, in the last stanza, of "with a blind brow." Furthermore, the "I don't" phrases emphatically illustrate the emptiness of the heart: "I don't feel"; "I don't want"; "I

don't think." The enjambement, especially in the third line of the first
stanza and the second line of the third stanza, leads one to an expecta-
tion and then immediately to the disappointment of that expectation—
"Hosts": heavenly? no, "of regrets"; "start": a new beginning? yes, but
the beginning, not of action, but of the end of action, "to sit." We be-
lieve that the poem is "real"—that is, that it is a direct and unmediated
expression of intense despair—at least partly because of the strength of
Berryman's craft. There is a distinction that must be made, even in these
late, personal poems, between poet and man, between maker and sub-
ject. Berryman the poet has not been subsumed by Berryman the man.
In all of these poems the emotion is worked, given form and order. Ber-
ryman was never a poet of "raw expression" (indeed, critics linking him
with the Beats have overlooked this obvious fact), and even in *Delu-
sions, Etc.* one must allow for the essential distinctions between the per-
sonality of the poet-in-the-poem and the personality of the poet. They
are not completely discontinuous, but neither are they identical, and it
is dangerous to argue across the barrier between them.

One fairly popular conception of the dangers inherent in confessional
verse is that the poet, by seeking out the unsettling and self-destructive
in himself, succeeds, not in controlling those feelings and putting them
to the service of his art, but in allowing those feelings to control him.
At least part of the responsibility for the rash of recent poet suicides,
then, is to be laid both to the type of material the poets were concerned
with and to the ultimate failure of their art. This might be true in certain
cases, and one may look at *Delusions, Etc.* in this manner, but such a
view would seem to me to be a great oversimplification. One must be
very careful of the post hoc fallacy here. The relation between life and
art—or at least Berryman's life and Berryman's art—is too complex to
fit such a matrix. I cannot prove this, of course. To do so it would be
necessary to conduct what scientists call a thought experiment—working
out in one's mind (or in computer simulation) all of the results of all of
the causes of both the life and the art. Nevertheless, I hope I have in-
dicated enough evidence of the complexity of the relationships between
Berryman's life and his art—even in these late poems—to call such a sim-
ple explanation into doubt.

There are both failures and successes of art in these late works. Despite
the successes, however, both *Delusions, Etc.* and *Love & Fame* are over-
shadowed by the accomplishments of *Homage to Mistress Bradstreet*
and *The Dream Songs*. It is hard to see how it could be otherwise. But
I cannot argue from the weaknesses of many of these poems to a failure
of life, or even a failure of talent, as many critics have—there are poems
enough here to attest to the continuance of Berryman's gift. Moreover,

what problems there are here are what might be termed positive problems—attempts to do with the language more than the language will successfully allow. Thus his failures here are not failures of character or even the failures of a dried-up talent, but those of the experimentalist that Berryman was until the end, pushing the language around at times quite roughly, to use it in ways in which it had not been used before.

NOTES

INTRODUCTION

1. Mary Doyle Curran, "Poems Public and Private," *Massachusetts Review* 6 (winter–spring 1965): 414.
2. Randall Jarrell, "Verse Chronicle," 81.
3. Peter Dale, "Slithy Tome," *Agenda* 9 (winter 1971): 52.
4. Ibid., 61.
5. Martin Dodsworth, "John Berryman: An Introduction," *The Survival of Poetry* (London: Faber and Faber, 1970), p. 119.
6. Ibid., p. 115.
7. J. K. Huysmans, *Against the Grain* (New York: Dover, 1931; reprinted 1969), p. 175.
8. "Olympus," *Love & Fame* (New York, 1970), p. 18.
9. Arthur Rimbaud, *Collected Poems,* trans. Oliver Bernard (Baltimore: Penguin Books, 1962), p. 13.
10. Reprinted in *Short Poems* (New York, 1962), p. 58.
11. Ibid., p. 13.
12. Ibid., pp. 29–30.
13. *Homage to Mistress Bradstreet,* stanza 39.

1: THE EARLY POEMS AND *THE DISPOSSESSED*

1. "Ars Poetica," *Columbia Poetry,* ed. Auslander (New York, 1935), p. 15.
2. "Note on E. A. Robinson," *Nation* 141 (10 July 1935): 38. The poem was reprinted in Auslander (ed.), *Columbia Poetry,* p. 14 and in the *Literary Digest* 121 (1 February 1936): 30.
3. In a review of Van Doren's *A Winter Diary, Columbia Review* 16 (April 1935): 42.

4. "E. A. Robinson, and Others," *Columbia Review*, 17 (December 1935): 20.
5. "A Note on Poetry,"*Five Young American Poets*, p. 47.
6. "The Heroes," *Love & Fame*, p. 26.
7. *The Autobiography of Mark Van Doren* (New York: Harcourt, Brace, 1958), p. 211. According to *Love & Fame*, of course, the young Berryman was not *solely* interested in verse.
8. "Shirley & Auden," *Love & Fame*, p. 7.
9. "Ars Poetica," p. 15.
10. *Columbia Review* 17 (April 1936): 7.
11. Berryman mentions the form in a review of *The World I Breathe*, in *Kenyon Review* 2 (autumn 1940): 483.
12. "One Answer to a Question," *Shenandoah* 17 (autumn 1965): 68.
13. Ibid., 70.
14. *Kenyon Review* 1 (summer 1939): 257–59. The poem was reprinted in *Five Young American Poets*, and, with revisions, in *The Dispossessed*.
15. "The Curse," *New Directions*, ed. James Laughlin, (Norfolk, Conn.: New Directions 1939), p. 126.
16. "Night and the City," *Five Young American Poets*, p. 66.
17. Ibid., p. 70.
18. "The Trial," ibid., p. 65.
19. "Caravan," ibid., p. 80.
20. Sigmund Freud, *Civilization and Its Discontents*, trans. James Strachey (New York: Norton 1962), p. 66.
21. "Desires of Men and Women," *Five Young American Poets*, p. 51.
22. Allen Tate, "The Last Omnibus," *Partisan Review* 81 (May–June 1941): 243.
23. "A Note on Poetry," p. 48.
24. Randall Jarrell, "In All Directions," *Partisan Review* 9 (July 1942): 347.
25. *Poems*, copyright page.
26. Ibid., p. 24.
27. Ibid., p. 11.
28. Ibid., pp. 12–13.
29. Ibid., p. 21.
30. "The Poetry of Ezra Pound," 384.
31. *The Dispossessed*, p. vii.
32. *Civilization and Its Discontents*, p. 92.
33. "The State of American Writing, 1942," 857.
34. *The Dispossessed*, pp. 102–3.
35. Ibid., p. 67.
36. *Civilization and Its Discontents*, p. 80.
37. *The Dispossessed*, pp. 24–25.
38. "The Imaginary Jew," 539.
39. *The Dispossessed*, p. 14.
40. "One Answer," 70.
41. *The Dispossessed*, 72–73.
42. "A Winter-Piece to a Friend Away," *The Dispossessed*, p. 96.
43. "The Lightning," *The Dispossessed*, p. 84.
44. Ross, Berryman, Tate, *The Arts of Reading*, p. 345.
45. "The Lovers," *Kenyon Review* 7 (winter 1945): 5.

46. *Civilization and Its Discontents*, p. 27n.
47. *The Dispossessed*, p. vii.
48. "One Answer," 70.
49. William J. Martz, *John Berryman*, pp. 17–18.
50. Randall Jarrell, "Verse Chronicle," 81.
51. "The Poetry of Ezra Pound," 388.

2: *BERRYMAN'S SONNETS*

1. Meredith's discussion can be found in the *Harvard Advocate* 103 (spring 1969): 19–22. J. M. Linebarger, in *John Berryman* (New York, 1974), adds further evidence, such as the date of the first sonic boom and the date of the first publication in English of Anne Frank's *Diary of a Young Girl.*
2. David McClelland et al., "An Interview with John Berryman," *Harvard Advocate* 103 (spring 1969): 7.
3. William Martz, *John Berryman*, p. 21.
4. Robert Mazzocco, "Harlequin in Hell," 14.
5. Ibid.
6. Ross, Berryman, Tate, *The Arts of Reading*, p. 346.
7. Ibid.
8. Berryman, *Short Poems*, p. 70.
9. Berryman, *Stephen Crane*, p. 214.
10. Berryman, "The Poetry of Ezra Pound," 386.
11. Reprinted in *Short Poems*, p. 28.
12. M. L. Rosenthal, *The New Poets*, p. 118. As Mr. Rosenthal is himself quick to point out, the widespread use of the term "confessional poetry" has caused "a certain amount of damage" (p. 25).
13. *Homage to Mistress Bradstreet*, stanzas 34–35.
14. McClelland et al., 7.
15. Tristan Corbiere, *Les Amours jaunes*, trans C. F. MacIntyre (Berkeley and Los Angeles: University of California Press, 1954), p. 68. This is the most readily available edition of Corbière's work.
16. Ibid., p. 72.

3: *HOMAGE TO MISTRESS BRADSTREET*

1. Steven Suppan, "Tales of an Editor," *Minnesota Daily* (8 October 1973), p. 11.
2. Peter Stitt, "The Art of Poetry XVI," 195–98.
3. The words are found in sonnet 46 and stanza 32 of *Mistress Bradstreet.*
4. Berryman, "One Answer to a Question," 73.
5. *Homage to Mistress Bradstreet*, note to 1.5.
6. See Alan Holder, "Anne Bradstreet Resurrected," *Concerning Poetry* 2 (spring 1969): 11–18, for a fuller discussion of the historical Bradstreet in relation to Berryman's poem.
7. Jeanine Hensley (ed.), *The Works of Anne Bradstreet* (Cambridge, Mass: Harvard University Press, 1967), p. 243.

8. See, for example, the *Paris Review* interview, p. 195.
9. "One Answer," 73.
10. Jonathan Sisson, "My Whiskers Fly," *Ivory Tower* (3 October 1966), p. 16.
11. "One Answer," 73.
12. Virginia Prescott Clark, "The Syntax of John Berryman's *Homage to Mistress Bradstreet,* p. 45.
13. John Ciardi, "The Researched Mistress," *Saturday Review* 40 (23 March 1957): 36.
14. "One Answer," 73.
15. Hensley (ed.), p. 241.
16. "One Answer," 74.
17. Ibid.
18. Ibid.

4: *THE DREAM SONGS*

1. Berryman, "One Answer to a Question," 74.
2. Ibid., 75.
3. Peter Stitt, "The Art of Poetry XVI," 193.
4. Berryman, *Stephen Crane,* p. 309.
5. David McClelland et al., "An Interview with John Berryman," *Harvard Advocate* 103 (spring 1969): 6.
6. Berryman, "The Curse," in *New Directions,* ed. James Laughlin (Norfolk, Conn.: New Directions, 1939), p. 126.
7. Anon., "Zoo-Maze: The World in Vaudeville," *TLS* (15 April 1965), p. 292.
8. Christopher Ricks, "Recent American Poetry," 336.
9. William Wasserstrom, "Cagey John," 338.
10. Norman Gottwald, *Studies in the Book of Lamentations,* rev. ed. (London: S. C. M. Press, 1962), p. 35. I don't know what "Gottwald & Co." in song 3 refers to. It could be Norman Gottwald, making the term refer to theologians and biblical scholars. This book was originally published in 1954, so it is entirely possible that Berryman was aware of it quite early on.
11. Ibid., p. 106.
12. Stitt, 203–4.
13. *Homage to Mistress Bradstreet,* 35.1–4.
14. John Haffenden (ed.), "Dream Songs," *TLS* (14 February 1975), p. 161.
15. Arthur Rimbaud, *A Season in Hell* and *The Drunken Boat,* trans. Louise Varese (New York: New Directions, 1961), p. 17.
16. Carl Wittke, *Tambo and Bones* (Durham, N.C.: Duke University Press, 1930), pp. 24–25.
17. H. L. Mencken, *The American Language,* abridged by Raven I. McDavid, Jr. (New York: Alfred A. Knopf, 1963), p. 98.
18. J. K. Huysmans, *Against the Grain,* p. 175.
19. Randall Jarrell, "Verse Chronicle," 81.
20. Berryman, introduction to Thomas Nashe, *The Unfortunate Traveller,* p. 11.

21. Olive Schreiner, *The Story of an African Farm,* 2nd ed. (Boston: Little, Brown and Co., 1927), vii–viii.
22. See Wasserstrom, and Patricia Brenner, "John Berryman's *Dream Songs.*"
23. McClelland et al., p. 6.
24. Stitt, 191.
25. William Meredith, "Henry Tasting All the Secret Bits of Life," 28.
26. McClelland et al., p. 5.
27. Richard Kostelanetz, "Conversation with Berryman," 341.
28. Stitt, 191.
29. "Afterword," in Theodore Dreiser, *The Titan,* p. 506.

5: LATE POEMS

1. "Poet Berryman Killed in Plunge from Bridge," *Minneapolis Tribune,* 8 January, 1972, p. 3A, col. 2.
2. William Borders, "Berryman and Shapiro Share Award," *New York Times,* 6 January 1969, p. 36.
3. Peter Stitt, "The Art of Poetry, XVI," 200.
4. "Scholia to Second Edition," *Love & Fame,* 2nd ed. (New York: Farrar, Straus & Giroux, 1972), page unnumbered.
5. Ibid.
6. Jerome Mazzaro, "False Confessions," *Shenandoah* 22 (winter 1971), 86–88.
7. Robert Phillips, *The Confessional Poets* (Carbondale, Ill.: Southern Illinois University Press, 1973), p. 100.
8. *Love & Fame,* 1st ed., p. 24.
9. Marjorie Perloff, *The Poetic Art of Robert Lowell* (Ithaca, N.Y.: Cornell University Press, 1973), p. 76.
10. Ibid., p. 178.
11. Phillips, 103–4.
12. "Afterword," in Theodore Dreiser, *The Titan,* p. 506.
13. "Year's End, 1970," *New York Times,* 1 January 1971, p. 22.
14. *Delusions, Etc.,* p. 33.

SELECTED BIBLIOGRAPHY

This bibliography makes no attempt to be exhaustive; I have listed only those works which I have found to be of special interest or usefulness. Readers interested in more complete bibliographical information should consult the running bibliographies in *John Berryman Studies* as well as the following works:

Arpin, Gary Q. *John Berryman: A Reference Guide.* Boston: G. K. Hall & Co., 1976.

Kelly, Richard J. *John Berryman: A Checklist.* Metuchen, N.J.: Scarecrow Press, 1972.

Stefanik, Ernest C. "Bibliography: John Berryman Criticism." *West Coast Review* 8 (October 1973): 45–52.

———. *John Berryman: A Descriptive Bibliography.* Pittsburgh: University of Pittsburgh Press, 1974.

WORKS BY BERRYMAN: POETRY

"Twenty Poems." In *Five Young American Poets,* edited by James Laughlin. Norfolk, Conn.: New Directions, 1940.

Poems. Norfolk, Conn.: New Directions, 1942.

The Dispossessed. New York: Sloane, 1948.

Homage to Mistress Bradstreet. New York: Farrar, Straus and Cudahy, 1956.

His Thoughts Made Pockets & the Plane Buckt. Pawlet, Vermont: C. Fredericks, 1958.

77 Dream Songs. New York: Farrar, Straus & Giroux, 1964.

Short Poems. New York: Farrar, Straus & Giroux, 1967.

Berryman's Sonnets. New York: Farrar, Straus & Giroux, 1967.

His Toy, His Dream, His Rest. New York: Farrar, Straus & Giroux, 1968.

The Dream Songs. New York: Farrar, Straus & Giroux, 1969.

Love & Fame. New York: Farrar, Straus & Giroux, 1970. Revised edition, 1972.

Delusions, Etc. New York: Farrar, Straus & Giroux, 1972.

WORKS BY BERRYMAN: PROSE

"The Lovers" (story). *Kenyon Review* 7 (winter 1945): 1–11.

"The Imaginary Jew" (story). *Kenyon Review* 7 (autumn 1945): 529–39.

"The State of American Writing, 1948" (symposium). *Partisan Review* (August 1948): 855–60.

"The Poetry of Ezra Pound." *Partisan Review* 16 (April 1949): 377–94.

Stephen Crane. New York: Sloane, 1950. Reprinted Meridian Books, 1962. Page references in my text are to the reprint.

"Shakespeare at Thirty." *Hudson Review* 6 (summer 1953): 175–203.

The Arts of Reading (with Ralph Ross and Allen Tate). New York: Crowell, 1960.

Thomas Nashe, *The Unfortunate Traveller* (edition, with introduction). New York: Putnam, 1960.

"Thursday Out" (story). *Noble Savage* 3 (May 1961): 186–94.

"The Dispossessed." In *Poet's Choice,* edited by Paul Engle and Joseph Langland. New York: Dial, 1962, pp. 134–36.

"Afterword." In Theodore Dreiser, *The Titan.* New York: New American Library, 1965, pp. 503–11.

"One Answer to a Question." *Shenandoah* 17 (autumn 1965): 67–76. Reprinted as "Changes" in *Poets on Poetry,* edited by Howard Nemerov. New York: Basic Books, 1966.

Recovery. New York: Farrar, Straus & Giroux, 1973.

WORKS ABOUT BERRYMAN

Alvarez, A. *Beyond All This Fiddle.* London: Allen Lane, 1968.

Anon. "The Life of the Modern Poet." *Times Literary Supplement* (23 February 1973), pp. 193–95.

Brenner, Patricia Ann. "John Berryman's *Dream Songs:* Manner and Matter." Ph.D. dissertation, Kent State University, 1970.

Clark, Virginia Prescott. "The Syntax of John Berryman's *Homage to Mistress Bradstreet.*" Ph.D. dissertation, University of Connecticut, 1968.

Connelly, Kenneth. "Henry Pussycat, He Come Home Good." *Yale Review* 58 (spring 1969): 419–27.

Harvard Advocate 103 (spring 1969), passim. Special Berryman issue.

Heyen, William. "John Berryman: A Memoir and an Interview." *Ohio Review* 15 (winter 1974): 46–65.

Howard, Jane. "Whiskey and Ink, Whiskey and Ink." *Life* 63 (21 July 1967): 67–76.

Jarrell, Randall. "Verse Chronicle," review of *The Dispossessed. The Nation* 167 (17 July 1948): 80–81.

Johnson Carol. *Reason's Double Agents.* Chapel Hill, North Carolina: University of North Carolina Press, 1966.

Kostelanetz, Richard. "Conversation with Berryman." *Massachusetts Review* 11 (spring 1970): 340–47.

Lieberman, Laurence. "The Expansional Poets." *Yale Review* 57 (winter 1968): 258–71.

Lowell, Robert. Review of *77 Dream Songs. New York Review of Books* 2 (28 May 1964): 2–3.

–––. "For John Berryman." *New York Review of Books* 18 (6 April 1972): 3–4.

Martz, William J. *John Berryman.* Minnesota Pamphlets on American Writers, no. 85. Minneapolis: University of Minnesota Press, 1969. Revised, 1975.

Mazzocco, Robert. "Harlequin in Hell." *New York Review of Books* (29 June 1967), pp. 12–16.

Meredith, William. "Henry Tasting All the Secret Bits of Life: Berryman's *Dream Songs.*" *Wisconsin Studies in Contemporary Literature* 6 (winter–spring 1965): 27–33.

Patrick, W. B. "Berryman's *77 Dream Songs:* 'Spare Now a Cagey John / a Whilom.'" *Southern Humanities Review* 5 (spring 1971): 113–19.

Pearson, Gabriel. "John Berryman–Poet as Medium." *The Review* (April 1965): 3–17.

Rich, Adrienne. "Mr Bones, He Lives." *The Nation* 198 (25 May 1964): 538–40.

Ricks, Christopher. "Recent American Poetry." *Massachusetts Review* 11 (spring 1970): 313–38.

Rosenthal, M. L. *The New Poets.* New York: Oxford University Press, 1967.

Stefanik, Ernest C. "A Cursing Glory: John Berryman's *Love & Fame.*" *Renascence* 25 (summer 1973): 115–27.

Stitt, Peter A. "The Art of Poetry XVI." *Paris Review* 14 (winter 1972): 177–207.

–––. "Berryman's Vein Profound." *Minnesota Review* 7 (1967): 356–59.

Wasserstrom, William. "Cagey John: Berryman as Medicine Man." *Centennial Review* 12 (summer 1968): 334–54.

INDEX